Behavioural and emotional difficulties

IDENTIFYING AND SUPPORTING NEEDS • ACTIVITIES COVERING EARLY LEARNING GOALS • WORKING WITH PARENTS

DR HANNAH MORTIMER

Author
Dr Hannah Mortimer

Editor
Sally Gray

Assistant Editor
Saveria Mezzana

Series Designers
Sarah Rock/Anna Oliwa

Designer
Heather Sanneh

Illustrations
Ann Kronheimer

Cover artwork
Claire Henley

Acknowledgements

The publishers gratefully acknowledge permission to reproduce the following copyright material:

Irene Yates for the use of 'Not such a good morning' by Irene Yates © 2002, Irene Yates, previously unpublished.
Qualifications and Curriculum Authority for the use of extracts from the QCA/DfEE document *Curriculum Guidance for the Foundation Stage* © 2000, Qualifications and Curriculum Authority.

The publishers wish to thank the BBC for the Internet activity described on page 64 and to Swinton Playgroup for their idea on page 80. The photocopiable record forms on page 85 and 86 are reproduced by kind permission of NASEN whose address is on page 95. Every effort has been made to trace copyright holders and the publishers apologize for any inadvertent omissions.

Text © 2002, Hannah Mortimer
© 2002, Scholastic Ltd
Designed using Adobe Pagemaker

Published by Scholastic Ltd, Villiers House,
Clarendon Avenue, Leamington Spa, Warwickshire CV32 5PR

Visit our website at www.scholastic.co.uk

Printed by Alden Group Ltd, Oxford

4 5 6 7 8 9 0   3 4 5 6 7 8 9 0 1

British Library Cataloguing-in-Publication Data A catalogue record for this book is available from the British Library.

ISBN 0 439 01915 X

Behavioural and emotional difficulties

5 INTRODUCTION

9 THE LEGAL REQUIREMENTS

15 HELPING CHILDREN WITH BEHAVIOURAL AND EMOTIONAL DIFFICULTIES

PERSONAL, SOCIAL AND EMOTIONAL DEVELOPMENT
25 Puppet pranks!
26 It's a pogwog!
27 How does it feel?
28 Right or wrong?
29 Consequences
30 My turn, your turn
31 Fair share
32 Knowing me, knowing you
33 Minding myself
34 King of the castle

COMMUNICATION, LANGUAGE AND LITERACY
35 Old MacDonald's book
36 Libraries
37 Are you receiving me?
38 Traffic signals
39 Telephone talk
40 Big voice, little voice
41 Kind and gentle
42 Special time
43 I hear with my little ear
44 One fine day...

MATHEMATICAL DEVELOPMENT
45 Spin the plate
46 Dotty dominoes
47 Two little hands
48 My space
49 Three wobbly jellyfish
50 Long line
51 Body shapes
52 How old are you?
53 One, two, three... GO!
54 Five little millipedes

KNOWLEDGE AND UNDERSTANDING OF THE WORLD

55 At your service
56 My story
57 Timetable
58 At the vet's
59 Golden rules
60 Rain drain
61 Setting the boundaries
62 Treasure map
63 Friends and neighbours
64 Surfing

PHYSICAL DEVELOPMENT

65 Tumbling Ted
66 Disco doubles
67 Jumping Jacks
68 Speckled frogs
69 Superheroes
70 Sitting still
71 Circus capers
72 Treading carefully
73 Lying low
74 What goes in...

CREATIVE DEVELOPMENT

75 Boot prints
76 Lead the band
77 I hear thunder
78 The special place
79 Sticky fingers
80 Egg splats
81 Treasure chest
82 Letting it out
83 Jungle howls
84 Magic moments

PHOTOCOPIABLES

85 Individual education plan
86 Planning sheet
87 Not such a good morning
88 Big voice, little voice
89 Dotty dominoes
90 Celebration certificate
91 My story
92 Golden rules
93 Speckled frogs
94 Special things

95 Recommended resources

INTRODUCTION

Children whose behaviour is challenging can be difficult to include in activities. This book provides practical ideas about how to plan activities for everybody, which also encourage individual children to look, listen, join in and feel positive about themselves.

The aims of the series

There is now a new, revised *Code of Practice* for the identification and assessment of special educational needs, and this series, *Special Needs in the Early Years*, aims to provide guidance to early years practitioners on how to meet and monitor special educational needs (SEN) under the new Code.

The QCA document *Curriculum Guidance for the Foundation Stage* emphasizes the key role that early years practitioners play in identifying needs and responding quickly to them. While most of us feel that an inclusive approach is the best one for all the children concerned, we still need guidance on what an inclusive early years curriculum might actually 'look like' in practice.

The books in this series cover most kinds of special needs:
- behavioural and emotional difficulties
- speech and language difficulties
- learning difficulties
- physical and co-ordination difficulties
- autistic spectrum difficulties

- medical difficulties
- sensory difficulties.

The eighth book in the series forms a handbook for the whole series, called *Special Needs Handbook*. This provides general guidance and more detail on how to assess, plan for, teach and monitor children with SEN in early years settings.

Most groups will at some point include children who have behavioural and emotional difficulties. This book will help all early years professionals to recognize and understand such difficulties and to provide inclusive activities for them.

Market research has shown that behaviour problems are the greatest area of special needs that early years educators work with. It seems that most practitioners would welcome practical advice and guidelines for these children. The activities suggested in this book will encourage the children to behave appropriately, and will also help them to gain confidence and motivation in their learning.

How to use this book

Chapter 1 provides an introduction to your requirements under the revised *Code of Practice* for SEN as it relates to children who have behavioural and emotional difficulties. This brief guide is intended to be used alongside the series handbook.

The chapter also includes a reminder of the requirements of the Early Learning Goals (QCA), with particular reference to those in the area of Personal, social and emotional development. The need for Individual education plans for those children who have SEN are introduced and there is discussion about what it means to meet SEN in an inclusive way. Pointers for developing positive partnership and relationships with parents, carers, families and any outside agencies are given.

In Chapter 2, the needs of children who have behavioural and emotional difficulties are considered. Information about the kinds of conditions and behaviours covered in the book are given, as well as consideration of what these behaviours mean for the child and what the educational implications are. Ideas for promoting appropriate behaviours, linked to the early years curriculum are given. There is also discussion about ways of approaching inclusion without disrupting the other children in the group. The 'ABC' approach to behaviour management is explained and introduced.

The activity chapters

The six activity chapters are each linked to one of the QCA Areas of Learning: Personal, social and emotional development; Communication, language and literacy; Mathematical development; Knowledge and understanding of the world; Physical development and Creative development. Each chapter contains ten activities, each with a learning objective for all the children (with or without SEN) and an individual target for any child who might have any one of a range of behavioural or emotional difficulties. The activities will target different kinds of difficulties in the hope that early years workers will develop a flexible approach to planning inclusive activities, dipping into the ideas in these chapters. Each child is an individual and it is impossible to prescribe set activities to meet the precise needs of your setting and the child with SEN. Instead, it is suggested that you read through all the activities for their general ideas, and then dip into them flexibly as part of your general curriculum planning.

Each activity also provides information of the size of group, a list of what you need, a description of what to do, any special support that might be necessary for the child with SEN, ideas for extending the activity for more able children, and suggestions for links with parents and carers at home.

Though this book relates to the Early Years and SEN procedures followed in England, the general guidance on individual planning, positive behaviour management and activities will be equally relevant to early years workers in other countries.

How children's behaviour and emotions normally develop

Children have to learn a lot about behaving and coping in their first five years, and you will have children at many different stages in your setting. From the earliest stages, children are learning about the care and nurturing that a committed adult can give them. Those who have consistent and caring nurturing from their parents or carers tend to develop positive confidence and self-esteem the most quickly. But there may be many reasons why this care and consistency has not always been available.

Children also need to learn about friendship and understand what behaviours are helpful when making and keeping friends. The QCA curriculum guidelines spell out the typical Stepping Stones which

children need to pass through in order to develop the Personal, social and emotional Early Learning Goals by the time they reach the end of their Foundation Stage. At age three to five, children tend to progress from playing alone or with an adult to playing alongside other children in parallel and eventually playing co-operatively. They define 'friend' as someone they have played with a lot. Children also have to learn about sharing and turn-taking. These skills do not come 'ready-packaged': they need to be taught, supported and encouraged. There are many activities in this book for developing these.

Children from two to four are still learning what is acceptable behaviour and what is not. If a certain behaviour leads to benefits for the child, such as a tantrum leading to getting their own way, then they are bound to repeat that behaviour. Put in this light, solving behaviour problems becomes a matter of giving the child new experiences and teaching them how to behave in different ways.

At all times we must preserve the children's self-esteem and confidence. That is why the approaches we use for managing challenging behaviour are based on positive praise and encouragement. Some ideas for balancing this with the needs of all the children in the group are also provided in Chapter 2.

Using a wide variety of resources in your setting

The activities described in this book encourage you to make use of a wide range of resources and materials available in your setting. There are ideas for art and craft, story time, physical play, and exploring and finding out. Special use is made of circle-time approaches with young children, since these have been shown to be very effective in building children's self-esteem and confidence and in teaching them how to behave in a group. The author's own research has shown that using a regular music circle time can enhance looking, listening and behaviour,

both within the circle time and beyond, and many of the activities in this book use a musical approach too.

Links with home

All the activities in this book include ways of keeping closely in touch with home. By sharing activities with parents and carers, you are also helping the parents or carers of a child who has behavioural and emotional difficulties to follow approaches which will make everyone feel more encouraged at home. Do not underestimate the effect that quality play time at home can have in developing positive family relationships and encouraging better communication and behaviour. Your role in originating this or in providing helpful ideas for play can be an important trigger in starting a more positive spiral of behaviour in the child, both in your setting and at home.

At the same time, 'difficult behaviour' can sometimes be an awkward issue to discuss with parents and carers, and people tend to become quickly defensive or blaming. There are ideas for developing effective ways of communicating about behaviour in Chapter 1. You also need to know that children can learn to behave very differently at home and in your setting, and so this needs handling with sensitivity when sharing information between home and school.

Providing special support for children with behavioural and emotional difficulties

Children tend to develop emotional independence gradually. Very young children still need to feel that there is an interested adult that they can 'attach' to in an early years setting and, so long as this adult is nearby, they will develop the confidence to join in and try new activities. This is especially true for children with behavioural and

emotional difficulties, and you will find it helpful to allocate a 'key worker' who can befriend and support that child as they settle in. The more time the key worker can invest in developing a positive interest in the child, the more they will be able to challenge their relationship with the child by confronting them about difficult behaviours. The key worker can also come to know the child well enough to provide very consistent handling of their behaviour.

It is important to ensure that the child with SEN is accessing the full range of your early years provision. Clearly this cannot happen if the child is isolated in any way or withdrawn from the group regularly, and this is another reason for collecting ideas for inclusive group activities. 'Support' does not mean individual one-to-one attention. Instead, it can mean playing alongside a child or looking on so as to encourage positive behaviour, staying one step ahead of any problem times, and teaching the child social skills in small groups. There are suggestions for doing this in Chapter 2.

THE LEGAL REQUIREMENTS

This chapter explains the SEN *Code of Practice*, the requirements of the Early Learning Goals and why there is a need for individual education plans for SEN children. There is also practical advice on working with parents and carers and with outside agencies.

The SEN *Code of Practice*

The SEN *Code of Practice* is a guide for school governors, registered early years providers and Local Education Authorities about the practical help that they can give to children with special educational needs. It recommends that schools and early years providers should identify children's needs and work with parents and carers to take action to meet those needs as early as possible. The aim is to enable all pupils with SEN to reach their full potential, to be included fully in their school communities and to make a successful transition to adulthood.

SEN in the early years setting

In 1996, the DfEE stated that all pre-school providers in the voluntary and non-maintained sectors who registered to redeem vouchers should also have regard to the *Code of Practice*. This continues to be the case for groups registering with the Local Education Authority (LEA) under the Early Years and Childcare Development Plan. There is now a new, revised SEN *Code of Practice* and this is described more fully in the handbook accompanying this series, *Special Needs Handbook*.

So, what are the underlying principles for early years settings? All children have a right to a broad and balanced curriculum which enables them to make maximum progress towards the Early Learning Goals. Early years practitioners must recognize, identify and meet SEN within their settings. There will be a range of need and a range of provision to meet that need. Most children with SEN will be in a local mainstream early years group or class, even those who have 'statements of SEN'. Parents, children, early years settings, and support services should work as partners in planning for and meeting SEN.

Identifying and meeting needs

The *Code of Practice* is designed to enable SEN to be identified early and addressed. These needs will normally be met in the local mainstream setting, though some children may need extra consideration or help to be able to access the early years curriculum fully. There is more detailed information about your requirements under the SEN *Code of Practice* in the series handbook.

It is recognized that good practice can take many forms and early years providers are encouraged to adopt a flexible and a graduated response to the SEN of individual children. This approach recognizes that

there is a continuum of SEN and, where necessary, brings increasing specialist expertise on board if the child is experiencing continuing difficulties. Once a child's SEN have been identified, the providers should intervene through 'Early Years Action'. When reviewing the child's progress and the help that they are receiving, the provider might decide to seek alternative approaches to learning through the support of the outside support services. These interventions are known as 'Early Years Action Plus'.

Specialist support

Early Years Action Plus is characterized by the involvement of specialists from outside the setting. The Special Educational Needs Co-ordinator (SENCO) continues to take a leading role, working closely with the member of staff responsible for the child, and:

● draws on the advice from outside specialists, for example, Early Years Support Teachers, Educational Psychologists or Behavioural Support Teachers;
● ensures that the child and their parents or carers are consulted and kept informed;
● ensures that an individual behaviour plan (IBP) is drawn up, incorporating the specialist advice, and that it is included in the curriculum planning for the whole setting;
● monitors and reviews the child's progress with outside specialists;
● keeps the Head of the setting informed.

For a very few children, the help provided by Early Years Action Plus will still not be sufficient to ensure satisfactory progress. The provider, external professional, and parents or carers may then decide to ask the LEA to consider carrying out a statutory assessment of the child's SEN.

The LEA must decide quickly whether or not it has the evidence to indicate that a statutory assessment is necessary for a child. It is then responsible for co-ordinating a statutory assessment and will call for the reports that it requires: from the early years teacher; an educational psychologist; a doctor; the Social Services department (if involved), and will also ask the parents or carers to submit their own views and evidence. Once it has collected in this evidence, the LEA might decide to issue a 'statement of SEN' for the child. Only children with severe and long-standing SEN go on to receive a statement – about 2% of children. There are various rights of appeal in the cases of disagreement, and the LEA can provide information about these.

Requirements of the Early Learning Goals

Registered early years providers are also expected to deliver a broad and balanced curriculum across the six Areas of Learning, as defined in the *Curriculum Guidance for the Foundation Stage* (QCA). The establishment of these goals paved the way for Baseline Assessment measures on entry

to school (from September 1998) and into National Curriculum assessment for school-age children. It was expected that the integration of these three would contribute to the earlier identification of children who were experiencing difficulties in making progress.

The Early Learning Goals are intended to be put into context so that they are seen as an aid to planning ahead rather than as an early years curriculum to replace 'learning through play'. Effective early years education needs both a relevant curriculum and practitioners who understand and are able to implement it. To this end, practical examples of Stepping Stones towards the Early Learnign Goals are provided in the detailed curriculum guidance.

Within this book, each activity is linked to a learning objective for all the group, and also to an individual target for any child who has behavioural and emotional difficulties. You will find that many of these individual targets relate to the area of Personal, social and emotional development.

Quality provision

Defining a set of Early Learning Goals which most children will have attained by the end of their Foundation Stage (the end of their reception year) has helped to ensure that nursery education is of good quality and a sound preparation for later schooling.

Registered early years practitioners are required to have their educational provision inspected regularly. The nursery inspectors, appointed by the Office for Standards in Education (OFSTED), assess the quality of the early years educational provision; look at the clarity of roles and responsibilities within the setting; are interested in plans for meeting the needs of individual children (including those with SEN); and look at plans for developing partnership with parents and carers.

In Scotland, there is also a curriculum framework for three- to five-year-olds. Here, there are five key aspects of learning: Emotional, personal and social development (including religious and moral development), Knowledge and understanding of the world (including environmental studies and mathematics), Communication and language, Expressive and aesthetic development, and Physical development and movement. The activities within this book will also be relevant to these aspects.

The need for individual education plans

One characteristic of Early Years Action for the child with SEN is the writing of the individual education plan (IEP). This is a plan which should lead to the child making progress. When planning for a child who has behavioural and emotional difficulties, this might be called the individual behaviour plan (IBP). The book, *Developing Individual Behaviour Plans in Early Years Settings* by Hannah Mortimer (NASEN) (see page 95), is a useful resource when writing up such plans. The publishers, NASEN, produce a range of other useful publications on SEN and behaviour. The following is an example of an IEP. In addition, the photocopiable sheet on page 85 provides a useful proforma.

Individual education plan

Name: Daniel	**Stage:** 3

Nature of difficulty: Daniel has a very short attention span and finds it hard to play socially with other children without physically hurting them.

Action

1 Seeking further information

Greta will be Daniel's key worker. She will talk with his mum and find out which other services are involved. If there are other professionals working with Daniel's family, she will enquire about their approaches with Daniel so that we can follow through any effective strategies in pre-school.

2 Seeking training

We would like to learn more about helping Daniel to handle his tempers, develop more appropriate ways of interacting with other children, and play for longer, preferably with other children. James, our SENCO, will contact the LEA's Behaviour Support Service for information about any suitable training courses.

3 Assessing Daniel

We need a system of monitoring and recording Daniel's play and behaviour which fits in with our nursery activities. Greta will spend the first two sessions running an 'ABC' analysis of his behaviour. She will observe him as he plays, keeping running notes of all he does in clear, objective words. We will be able to see the **a**ntecedents to difficult behaviour, record the **b**ehaviour itself, and note the **c**onsequences of it for Daniel. Afterwards, we should have a record of both Daniel's strengths and weaknesses, which we can use to settle his behaviour and develop his skills.

4 Managing his behaviour

- Daniel will be given a high level of adult attention, which he seems to crave, but this will be when he is behaving appropriately. If he is feeling cross and stressed, Greta will invite him to sit quietly in the cushion corner with the music tapes, so that he feels calmer. Daniel should be allowed to go there if he feels the need.
- Whenever there are opportunities, Daniel should be shown how to play for longer, to share, to take turns and to share fun with other children appropriately.
- Whenever he moves to hit, kick, or bite another child, Greta will draw him away with a clear 'No biting, Daniel', and sit with him quietly on the cushions for a minute. She should then talk to Daniel about what he could have done differently, and help him to apologize or restore any damage.
- We will use circle time for choosing activities to boost Daniel's self-esteem and confidence within the group.

Help from parents

Daniel's mum, Jean, agrees to make a point of talking with Daniel's key worker, Greta, every Friday after pre-school. They will share the good news as well as the difficulties.

Targets for this term

- Daniel will play on the train mat for ten minutes, with other children playing alongside him in parallel.
- Daniel will play co-operatively with one other child for five minutes with Greta helping.
- Daniel will manage three sessions in a row without hitting, kicking or biting another child.
- Daniel will begin to look pleased when he is praised and begin to take pride in his achievements.

Review meeting with parents: In six weeks' time. Invite any other professional who is involved.

Working with parents and carers

Parents and carers are the primary educators of their children and should be included as an essential part of the whole-group approach to meeting a child's needs from the start. They have expert knowledge on their own children, and you will need to create an ethos which shows how much this information is valued and made use of. Information sharing is important and is a two-way process. Below are some practical ways of involving parents and carers in meeting their children's needs:

● Make a personal invitation to parents and carers to share information about their children's achievements, in an informal way, or to arrange a home visit if possible.

● Draw the parents and carers' attention to a display showing their children's work.

● Show parents and carers what their children have already achieved, and highlight improvements to their behaviour within your setting. Do not make them feel too despondent if there have not been improvements at home.

● Ask the children to show their parents or carers what they can do or have learned.

● Ask parents and carers for their opinions. It is often helpful to set a regular time aside when other demands will not intrude.

● Thank parents and carers regularly for their support.

● Celebrate success with parents and carers.

● Use home/school diaries to keep in touch if regular contact is difficult.

A two-way system of sharing information about a child's success, experiences and opportunities can help in supporting the child.

Working with outside agencies

At times, when assessing and working with a young child who has SEN, an outside professional is involved in helping to monitor and meet the

child's needs. Some children entering an early years setting may already be at this stage. The kinds of advice and support available will vary with local policies and practices.

Usually, a request for help from outside agencies is likely to follow a decision taken by the SENCO, colleagues and parents or carers when reviewing a child's progress in the setting. Has progress been made? What do the parents or carers feel? Do we need more information and advice on the child's needs from outside?

Developing inclusive practice

Inclusion is the practice of including all children together in a setting. All children participate fully in all the regular routines and activities of the classroom or playroom, though these might need to be modified to meet individual children's goals and objectives. This is why the activities in this book carry both learning objectives for *all* the children (with and without SEN) and individual targets for the child who has SEN.

The following are suggestions for factors that support inclusive practices:
● careful joint planning, especially to make sure that any within-class support is used effectively;
● the use of educational labels rather than categories or medical labels (such as 'behaviour difficulty' rather than 'conduct disorder', or even 'child who has SEN' rather than 'SEN child');
● teachers and adults who provide good role models for the children because of their positive expectations and the way they respect and value the children;
● the use of strategies which improve the children's communication and behaviour;
● the use of teaching strategies which enable *all* children to participate and to learn;
● individual approaches which draw on pupils' earlier experiences, set high expectations and encourage mutual peer support;
● the flexible use of support aimed to promote joining in and inclusion rather than to create barriers and exclusion.

In addition to these ideas, you may find the publication by Sebba and Sachdev useful (see page 96).

HELPING CHILDREN WITH BEHAVIOURAL AND EMOTIONAL DIFFICULTIES

Young children are at many different stages of development, understanding and experience.

The behaviours covered

This book talks of 'difficult behaviours' and not 'difficult children'. If there is a 'problem behaviour', it does not follow that there is a 'problem child'. There may be many reasons why a child is behaving in a certain way, and the main reasons are that a child has not yet learned how to behave appropriately; a child's social skills are still immature; or a child's self-esteem and ability to form relationships are poor. Almost every child is described by at least one adult as 'having behaviour problems' in some situation or other and at some stage of their first five years. Readers will find the book *Developing Individual Behaviour Plans in Early Years Settings* by Hannah Mortimer (NASEN) (see page 95) useful and this chapter summarizes its approach.

The prevalence and causes

Children's behaviour depends on the developmental stage they have reached and the particular experiences they have had. Perhaps they are still at a very early stage in learning to concentrate, to look and listen and this is why they do not do as they are asked. Perhaps they do not understand abstract words like 'gentle' or 'naughty' and your very words and instructions are 'overloading' them with language they do not understand. For some children, separating from home might still be traumatic, or they may lack experience and confidence when adjusting to new people or places. Perhaps they are still at a stage of needing to explore and to touch everything. Perhaps the very idea of 'rules' is new to them and they have yet to learn that 'no' means 'no' or that playing socially involves a degree of turn-taking and sharing.

In this light, behaviour which might at first seem 'inappropriate' can be understood differently.

Suddenly the adult's task becomes one of teaching new skills and inspiring new confidence, rather than just 'getting rid of' an inappropriate behaviour.

Desirable behaviour

If we are going to speak of 'difficult' behaviours, it would be helpful to be clear about the behaviours we are hoping to encourage in early years settings. Here are some examples. We would like children to be able to:

● feel motivated and confident enough to develop to their best potential;
● to respect themselves and other people;
● to be able to make friends and gain affection;
● to express their feelings in appropriate ways;

● to 'do as they are nicely asked';
● to make a useful contribution to the group;
● to develop a positive self-esteem.

You will find Ann Henderson's book helpful here (see page 95). The Early Learning Goals for Personal, social and emotional development also describe the early years curriculum in this Area of Learning and are useful to refer to as skills to aim for by the end of the reception year.

How do we need to order the environment to make this likely?

Experience tells us that appropriate behaviour is most likely if children know what is expected of them. Some children may be coming to your setting with the idea that 'play' is synonymous with 'rough and tumble'. They may need to be shown how to play appropriately, and helped to understand the right and wrong times for more physical behaviour. They respond best to a familiar structure with a calm and purposeful atmosphere, but it may take them a while to become familiar with your routines and to understand that play can be purposeful and intrinsically rewarding.

Children also respond best where there is mutual courtesy, kindness and respect, making it easier for them to work and play together. Again, this might need to be learned in the context of your setting with the adults constantly modelling courteous and kind behaviour to one another and to the children. 'Please' and 'thank you' come much more easily when they are part of the daily exchange between all people at your setting and at home than when the children are confronted with constant demands to 'say the magic word'.

Appropriate behaviour is also more likely if positive approaches are used to raise and maintain the children's self-esteem. Children who are 'nagged' constantly with 'don't' and 'no' tend to stop listening or trying after a while, and come to see themselves as 'naughty'. Children whose appropriate behaviour is noticed and praised are more likely to repeat the behaviours which are attracting your admiration, and to see themselves as helpful and kind. Remarks such as 'Good to see you sharing the tea set, Tara' are encouraging and rewarding.

Positive encouragement

Confidence and learning seem to be bound together: if a child tries something new and fails, their self-esteem and self-confidence become lower and they are less likely to try again. If a child tries something new and succeeds, self-esteem and confidence are raised, and they are likely to try again next time. That is why it is so important that the approaches we design for helping children's behaviour to change should remain positive and should leave the child feeling good about themselves. Negative approaches might control a situation in the short-term, but can only leave the child feeling worse about themselves in the longer-term.

Deciding if there is a problem

If you have a child in your setting whose behaviour is causing concern, ask yourself the questions below before you decide on whether there might be the need for special approaches:

● Has the child had time to settle into your group? Some children take longer than others to settle into new routines.

● Talk with parents and carers; they can contribute useful information and ideas. What they say might allay your fears or lead you to using more special approaches.

● Have you considered that poor self-esteem and confidence might be at the root of things? If so, use a key worker to befriend and support the child.

● Has the child not yet learned to play calmly and socially? This might not be a 'behaviour problem', but more a case of teaching the child another way to play and behave. Look for strategies to make play extra fun, and rules clear.

● Is the child at a developmental stage where he or she has learned sharing, turn-taking and other such appropriate behaviours? It might be

that the 'behaviour problem' can be related to the fact that the child is still at a young stage of development.

● Choose a few clear rules that the children have contributed to in your setting. Talk about them at circle time. Look for opportunities to praise the children specifically for following the rules. Help the children who did not by showing them what to do instead, and then praising them for doing it.

If the child has had time to settle with you and is not responding to your usual encouragement and boundary setting despite all the approaches above, then

consider talking to the parents or carers about more special approaches. Consider also entering the child's name on your special needs register and putting together a within-setting individual behaviour plan as described in Chapter 1 (see also page 85).

Looking for opportunities to change behaviour

The best way to change a child's behaviour is to change what you are doing. Here are a few suggestions.

Avoid likely situations

If a child cannot sit still during a story, avoid that situation for the time being while you concentrate on teaching them to look and listen with one adult in the book corner.

Distract rather than confront

'Please don't draw on the wall, here's some paper to draw on instead'. Remember when giving verbal instructions that some children might only register certain key words. The fact that they have complied does not mean that they have understood everything you have said. Try to keep instructions and feedback simple, and be aware that if the child does not comply, it might be that they have not fully understood you.

Make sure that the activity suits the child's level

So often, children who are having behaviour difficulties turn out to be experiencing difficulties in learning as well. When children cannot succeed in their learning, they sometimes 'save face' by distracting others or avoiding the learning situation altogether. Make sure that the child is bound to succeed in each activity you set, even if you are doing so through the help and support you are giving.

Get full attention before giving directions

If necessary, bend down to the child's level, say their name, or gently touch their chin to ensure eye contact before you give instructions. Young children find it hard to realize that instructions given to a whole group also include *them* so cue in individual children first to what you are about to say.

Give more positive attention before the trouble happens

Some children who appear to *seek* a lot of attention genuinely *need* a great deal of positive attention. Look for ways of providing that attention when they are behaving appropriately (they do not have to be *extra* good) and target your praise specifically.

Give a warning of changes of activity

Young children get engrossed in what they are doing and have not learned to attend to more than one thing at a time. Give a warning

such as 'In five minutes it will be time to tidy up'. Remember that some children will find it hard to understand how long five minutes is.

Anticipate problem times and be a step ahead
Difficult behaviours often occur when children are in between activities or waiting for something to happen. Make sure that each child knows not only what they can be doing now, but what they can do next.

Relate to a child's particular needs
Other difficult times may relate to a child's particular needs. Children with language and social difficulties find 'free play' difficult because they are not sure what might be expected of them. Children with difficulties in attention will find sitting still for long periods challenging, and find it easier if they can sandwich 'doing' and 'letting off steam'. Get to know the individual child's needs and try to see your session from their point of view, avoiding the difficult times of day.

Give clear directions
We know that children need full reasons and explanations if they are to learn about their worlds, yet there may be times when that is not appropriate. Choose what you want to say, for example, 'No kicking' and repeat that over, making your rule simple and clear. The more you elaborate, the more attention you are giving the child for behaving inappropriately. Instead, look for other times of day when you can talk together about reasons and learn about behaving kindly.

Show the child what to do as well as saying it
Young children are usually too absorbed in what they are doing to respond to your directions from across the room. You will need to approach them and model what to do.

Choose a few simple rules and stick to them
These are especially useful when your children have contributed to them too – perhaps as a circle-time activity. Try to stick to three to four rules at the most, perhaps relating to not hurting others, to being kind and to listening. Take time to talk together about what it means to be kind and to help.

Stop the behaviour if you can
Children in early years settings are still small enough for you to be able to gently withdraw a child from trouble where and when you have to.

Teach the child a new behaviour opposite to the first
If a child's enjoyment and understanding of 'playing' is to physically tackle another child, then you need to introduce new repertoires of

playing for that child and show that they, too, can be exciting and pleasurable. You can also teach the children social skills, such as giving a toy or biscuit to another child.

Praise another behaviour incompatible with the first

Perhaps the child already has different ways of playing; praise and encourage the appropriate ways and discourage the inappropriate ones.

Be absolutely consistent

If a child learns, through constant tantrums, that there might be the occasional time when you *will* give in, perhaps on the day of an inspection or when you are feeling particularly stretched, then they have learned to tantrum longer and louder until you eventually give in. At first, every incident of the inappropriate behaviour needs dealing with, just as every example of appropriate behaviour needs encouraging and praising. Consider allocating time from a key worker to be extra vigilant while you introduce an individual behaviour plan. This should not be for long; once the child is learning new patterns of behaviour, you will be able to step back and reward or praise them less frequently.

Ignore attention-seeking behaviour where safe to do so

This is difficult in front of an audience of interested young eyes. You may need to withdraw with the child away from the attention, wait for any tantrum to subside without giving further attention of your own, and then help the child to say 'sorry' or restore any damage.

Make it fun to behave appropriately

Behaving in an inappropriate way might have become a habit for the child and you will need to make your rewards and praise particularly strong to break the pattern. Make sure that your praise is attention-getting, immediate and easy to use (a trip to the park much later is not). Pair all concrete praise (such as a favourite toy to play with) with your verbal praise as well, so that eventually the child will find praise rewarding in itself.

Star charts and stickers can also work well

Try not to overuse these. Make sure the child knows exactly why they have earned a sticker. Never remove it once given, whatever the child does next. Stickers are a concrete sign that the child has behaved in an appropriate way at that particular moment, and help them to learn that you have praised them because *they* did something, not because *you*

decided to be pleased with them. You will find some useful addresses on page 96.

Approaching inclusion without too much disruption

You need to take care that the child's individual behaviour programme is integrated into your short-, medium- and long-term curriculum planning for the whole group. While you should not use a key worker to constantly 'shadow' or withdraw a child, they can provide a pair of vigilant eyes which help you to stay one step ahead of trouble. They can also provide support for a small group of children when the targeted child is still learning to take turns or to share.

Having a key worker allocated to a child means that you can swing into a well-discussed and planned intervention if the child's behaviour becomes disruptive or dangerous to the other children. The key worker can quietly withdraw the child away from the audience and sit with them, giving minimal attention, until things have calmed down. The child can then be helped to put things right or apologize. You might find the individual behaviour plan on page 85 helpful here.

Trying a range of approaches

Throughout the activities, you will find suggestions for approaches which have been effective for 'real' children. It is impossible to prescribe what is going to work for your children and situation. Instead, develop your activities flexibly, dipping into the suggestions which you anticipate will be effective for your particular circumstances. It helps to have a clear individual behaviour plan in mind which you are all working towards for a particular child (see Chapter 1 and page 85).

How can you gather the information you need to put together your IBP, and how do you plan a behavioural approach for changing the child's behaviour? Here are a few suggestions.

The ABC approach

The 'ABC' approach to behaviour management described below is based on the theory of behavioural psychology. The approach depends on the use of positive encouragement and reward. In essence, a behavioural theory states:

● If we do something, and something *pleasant* happens to us, we are more likely to do that thing again.

● If we do something, and something *unpleasant* happens to us, we are less likely to do that thing again.

● The *pleasant* event is called a 'reward', simply because it makes the behaviour increase.

● The *unpleasant* event is called a 'punishment', simply because it makes the behaviour decrease.

● Punishments need not be something unpleasant that happens; they can simply be that

the child was expecting a certain reward to happen and it never did (for example, the temper tantrum did not bring the expected tractor ride).

The approaches described in this book also lean on what we know about the development of self-esteem and children's early attachments. We know from research that:

● children with warm, affectionate relationships with their parents or carers generally have high self-esteem;

● children with a high self-esteem are more likely to view others positively;

● children with high self-esteem are going to find it easier to make friends;

● children with a positive image of themselves are likely to be more independent, more likely to achieve academically and to be better socially adjusted;

● older children who view themselves and others positively are more likely to take a stand against discrimination;

● positive approaches to managing difficult behaviour help to ensure that the child's self-esteem remains intact.

Gathering information: talking with parents and carers

Talking with parents and carers becomes easier if you have shared a relationship from the start – sharing good news as well as bad. Get to know the child and parent or carer before the starting date, preferably through a home visit so they see you on home ground. Take time to find out about the child's likes and dislikes, and what motivates him or her – this can provide you with valuable information to help you settle the child over the first few days. Once the child has started going to your setting, find something positive to say to the parents or carers about their child each session. It can be very daunting to be spoken to only when the news is 'bad'. It can also be disconcerting if parents and carers are told nothing of the difficulties until they have really escalated, because of fear of worrying them. This is best tackled by finding ways of rephrasing behaviours into positive terms, for example, 'Stuart seems happy here but finds it hard to share; how have you found things when he plays with other children at home?'.

Gathering information: observing the behaviour

To change a difficult behaviour into a more appropriate one, you need to know where you started from and when you have 'got there'. Your starting-point is called the 'baseline'. It gives you a clear picture of how difficult or frequent the behaviour was before you started your plan to change things. You can measure behaviour in different ways.

Observation

Observe the target child for part of a session – arrange the staffing so that you can be released. Make it clear to colleagues that you would like

to be a 'fly on the wall' and not be involved at all with the running of the session. They should be responsible for managing all behaviour in the group and do the same things they would normally do. Sit at the edge of the room with a pad and pen. Keep your eyes down when curious children approach. Tell them briefly but pleasantly that you are 'doing your writing today', and do not be drawn into eye contact or involvement with them.

Keep a running record of everything that the target child does. Do not write your impressions ('he seems to be unhappy now') but write down clearly exactly what you can see and hear ('she is throwing the doll down') so that anyone reading your notes would have a mental picture of what was going on. In the margin, write the time down every five minutes so that you have an idea of how long the child spent on each activity.

Because you are recording everything that the child does, as each 'behaviour' unravels, you will have running notes of:
- the Antecedent to the behaviour (what led up to it);
- the Behaviour itself (describe this clearly);
- the Consequences (what happened next).

This will allow you to carry out an 'ABC' analysis, by looking at the behaviour itself, as well as the antecedents and the consequences surrounding that behaviour. It has the advantage of giving you much information about the child's strengths and interests as well as the difficult behaviours.

Keeping a diary

You can also carry out an 'ABC' analysis by recording isolated events in the form of a diary. Decide with colleagues what the difficult behaviour that you are going to measure is, defining it in clear terms. Words like 'aggressive', 'temper tantrum' or 'naughty' are open to many

interpretations – instead, describe what the child is actually doing, such as 'biting' or 'throwing'. Record the time of day, what the child did, what led up to it and what happened as a result. With certain behaviours, you could measure how often they happen, for example, 'six incidents of trying to bite another child'. Sometimes, it is possible to measure the amount of time a child is doing something; 'she spends a fifth of the session playing alongside another child, and the rest of the time she is isolated'.

Now you are ready to collect together the information you need for your IBP (see the photocopiable sheet on page 85).

Using the 'ABC' analysis to change the difficult behaviour

1. Select just one behaviour to work on first:
- one that is easy to change;
- or one which is causing the most disruption.

You cannot change everything at once. Some behaviours (like swearing) are difficult to change, others need your immediate attention because they affect other people (like hitting) or endanger the child (like running away).

2. Decide on a hypothesis:
● What do you think is keeping that behaviour going?

This will give you the opportunity to devise a plan for intervention which you can then evaluate and redesign if you seem to be on the wrong track. You might decide that the child is behaving in the way they are because, for example, they are seeking attention.

3. Draw up a plan to change the A, the B or the C.
● What sort of interventions can you use to change antecedents, behaviours or consequences? The most common and effective approaches were described above. Perhaps you can apply several interventions at once. It is usually helpful when designing approaches to change inappropriate behaviour to teach another behaviour in its place. That way, the child not only learns what not to do, but what they could be doing instead.

It is helpful for consistency and the child's self-esteem if one key worker is involved in seeing the behavioural approach through. That key worker will need regular support from the SENCO, head teacher or group leader. It can soon feel very 'personal' when a child does not

respond immediately to intervention, and ongoing support and reassurance is needed. Above all, you need to feel confident that it is safe for you to go on managing the behaviour consistently, even if the behaviour seems to get initially worse. If there is any element of attention-seeking in the behaviour, it is bound to become worse before it eventually improves, since boundaries will be sought and stretched to their limits before the behaviour settles.

It is imperative, in the interest of preserving the child's self-esteem, that the child comes to know that it is the *behaviour* that is unacceptable rather than they themselves as an individual child. The same key worker who is responsible for managing the behaviour programme should also be on hand to play alongside the child and encourage them, and to give more positive attention to their appropriate behaviours than negative attention to the inappropriate ones. Instructions need to be delivered to the child neutrally, without any hint of impatience or anger – that is, as facts rather than as emotional threats.

The series handbook, *Special needs handbook*, explains how to evaluate the success of your individual plan, how to monitor the child's progress and how to review this with the parents or carers.

PERSONAL, SOCIAL AND EMOTIONAL DEVELOPMENT

This chapter provides activities that encourage all the children's personal, social and emotional development. Ideas are given to support children with behavioural and emotional difficulties.

LEARNING OBJECTIVE FOR ALL THE CHILDREN
● to maintain attention when doing a practical activity.

INDIVIDUAL BEHAVIOUR TARGETS
● to watch closely and to imitate for five turns of a turn-taking game
● to link the word 'gentle' to actions.

Puppet pranks!

Group size
Two to three children.

What you need
A selection of glove puppets.

What to do
Gather the children around and show them the puppets. Encourage them to try the puppets on and to choose one. Explain that you are going to play a game of copying. Can the children make their puppets do just what yours does? Tell the 'puppets' to try not to touch

one another while they copy. Make your puppet dance or go to sleep. Make it lift up one arm, jump in the air or fly. Pause between each action to praise the puppets for copying and to make each action distinct from the last. After four or five 'turns', ask one of the puppets to choose an action for the others to copy. Allow the puppets to take turns. Praise the puppets for looking carefully. Now invite the puppets to hold hands. Stand in a circle as you very gently make the puppets touch hands until they are all in a ring. Finish with a peaceful 'dance' as they touch hands. Praise them for being 'gentle'.

Special support
Work on a one-to-one basis with children who have attention difficulties or who find it hard to take turns. Try to build up to five turns as you make your puppet perform an action for the child to copy with their puppet, and you then copy theirs. Now introduce the word 'gentle' as your puppet gently touches the child's nose, and their puppet touches yours. Again, continue this for four or five 'turns'.

Involve one other child on the next occasion that you do this activity. Gradually build up the size of the group until the child is turn-taking gently with two or three other children.

Extension
Encourage older children to take the lead so that you can copy.

LINKS WITH HOME
Ask parents and carers to practise gentle games at home by asking their children to cuddle a teddy and so on. Encourage them to praise their children for being gentle.

LEARNING OBJECTIVE FOR ALL THE CHILDREN

● to maintain attention, concentrate and sit quietly when appropriate.

INDIVIDUAL BEHAVIOUR TARGET

● to listen to and remember what is said.

It's a pogwog!

Group size
Six children.

What you need
A bag; selection of six unusual or interesting objects which are easy to handle, such as a loofah, a soft toy, a wooden spoon and so on.

What to do
Hide your selection of items in the bag. Gather the children in a circle and sit together on the floor, ensuring that your targeted child is sitting to your left. Explain to the children that you are going to show them some interesting things and that you are all going to try to make up names for them.

Bring out the first object and show it to the child on your left. Say to him or her, 'This is a pogwog', then ask, 'What is it?'. Encourage the child to reply 'pogwog' and invite them to show it to the next child in the circle, saying its name as they pass it. Each time, add the question 'What is it?' and enjoy the refrain as the children give you the right answer back.

When you have passed the item all around the circle, return it to the bag and choose a new item. Pass it to your right and make up a new name for it.

Invite the children, in turn, to choose an item to pass around. Invite them to think of a name for it (making sure it is suitable).

Special support
Say the words for any children who are able to join in by passing the object but not speaking. If a child tries to take control of everybody, invite them to listen carefully to see if everyone is saying the right name. Praise them for sitting still and helping.

If a child kicks out or is aggressive, remove everybody's shoes for circle time and sit on a soft carpet with cushions. Involve an additional adult to cradle and support the child, encouraging them constantly and praising any calmness.

If a child shouts out very loudly, ignore it if you can and praise those who are speaking more quietly.

Extension
Involve older children in choosing the items and helping you to think of some funny names for them.

LINKS WITH HOME
Ask parents and carers to help their children choose an unusual object to bring in. Suggest that the children try to remember what it is called to tell everyone at circle time.

How does it feel?

Group size
Three or four children.

What you need
The story on the photocopiable
sheet on page 87.

What to do
Sit with the children in your story
corner and make yourselves
comfortable. Show the children the
illustration to the story and ask them
what they think is happening. Spend
a few moments following up their
ideas and introduce or emphasize
any words to do with feelings such
as 'angry', 'sad', 'upset' or
'frightened'.

Now read the story to the
children. Share Eysha's amazement
at what has happened. Did Eli mean
to do it? How does Eysha feel? What
do you think will happen next? Was
it an accident? If Eli did it by
accident, would that be all right?
Why do you think Eli did it on
purpose? What will the teacher say?
How can she help make things better? Do you think they could share
the train? How would they all feel then?

Agree an ending to the story together. Talk about sharing and ask the
children for examples of how this can be done. What are rules? Can the
children think of a good rule to make sure that they do not upset one
another and that everybody feels happy?

Special support
Follow up the story later in the session, relating it to any event of
aggressive behaviour. Talk again about feelings.

Make sure that you always see who has offended whom during the
session, so that you do not always assume that one child is the offender
and the others the victims. There are often other children who know
just how to provoke a child who tends to over-react. Again, talk quietly
to those involved, share feelings and look for ways of apologizing and
putting the situation right.

Draw a simple sign to represent your 'rule' about kindness or sharing.
Point to it discreetly when you need to remind a child.

Extension
Encourage older children to think of other examples of how children
can upset one another at nursery.

**LEARNING
OBJECTIVE FOR ALL
THE CHILDREN**
● to develop respect
for their own and
others' feelings.

**INDIVIDUAL
BEHAVIOUR TARGET**
● to use appropriate
words to describe
their feelings and to
begin to see that
others have feelings
too.

LINKS WITH HOME
Give each child a
copy of the story to
take home and ask
them to retell the
story and its ending
to their parents or
carers, talking about
how everybody felt.

Right or wrong?

Group size
Five or six children.

What you need
Three different soft toys; bag for one of the soft toys; small sweet to go in the bag.

What to do
Start this activity individually with the child that you are targeting. Ask them to help you get ready for a story by choosing three of the soft toys to take part. Choose one as the main character, one as a kind toy and one as a naughty toy. Ask the child to think of names for the characters. Invite them to hold on to the kind one for the first part of the story.

Gather the children in a circle and sit together on the floor. Introduce the three toys and ask your young helper to say their names. Place the little bag around the main character of your story, showing the children what is inside it.

Tell a story of the toy walking to nursery one day, making it do the actions. Talk about what it sees on its way as it looks all around. 'Oh dear! One of the toys has come up, stolen the sweet from the bag and has run away! When the first toy stops to have a snack, it finds that the sweet has gone. What will it feel like now? Look! It's crying. Was it right to take the sweet? Why? Here comes another toy to help.'

Encourage the child holding the third toy to make suggestions about how it will comfort and help the one which is crying. Ask the group quesitons such as, 'What can the toy that was naughty do to apologize?', 'What does it mean to "steal" something?', 'Is it right or wrong?' and so on.

Special support
If the children in your group often take things which do not belong to them, use this story to illustrate the reasons why it might be wrong.

Give clear information about what the children *can* take home (pictures, models and so on) and those they cannot (other children's belongings, group property and so on).

Extension
Ask older children to invent other scenarios of 'right' and 'wrong'.

LEARNING OBJECTIVE FOR ALL THE CHILDREN
● to understand what is right, what is wrong, and why.

INDIVIDUAL BEHAVIOUR TARGET
● to recognize appropriate behaviour.

LINKS WITH HOME
Tell parents and carers that you have been talking about 'right' and 'wrong' today. Ask them to help their children to think of one thing which is right and one thing which is wrong. Encourage the children to tell it to the group the next day.

Consequences

Group size
Four or five children.

What you need
A glove puppet for each child and for yourself.

What to do
Think of examples of hurtful things you have heard the children say to one another (without referring to specific children and situations, and avoiding repeating swear words). Sit down together and let each child choose a puppet. Help the puppets to 'make friends' with one another and 'play' happily. What are the puppets doing to make one another happy? Now make your own puppet turn to the others and say, 'I hate you all! I think you're all horrible and you smell!' (or use a real example). How are the puppets feeling now? Ask the children, 'Was that a good thing to say?' and 'Are your puppets going to want to play with mine now?'. Gather ideas for resolving the situation in a friendly way.

Talk about things that are kind to say and things that upset others. Follow up by praising the children individually whenever you hear them saying kind words.

Special support
Support the children as they apologize. Help them to think of kind words that they could use instead. Talk about how the other child feels.

If a child swears a lot, ignore what you can and praise the child for talking appropriately. If everyone else is reacting to a child's swearing, spend time individually with the child explaining which words can be used in the group and which cannot. Explain what 'swearing' means. Help the child to find a nonsense word for expressing themselves instead. Praise them whenever they are not swearing a lot.

Extension
Encourage older children to invent new behaviour for their puppets to illustrate kind behaviour and behaviour which upsets others.

LEARNING OBJECTIVE FOR ALL THE CHILDREN
● to consider the consequences of their words.

INDIVIDUAL BEHAVIOUR TARGET
● to talk about other children's responses to their behaviour.

LINKS WITH HOME
If a child swears a lot, talk to their parents or carers. Explain to the children that you would like to help *all* of them not to swear (so nobody feels singled out). Share the nonsense word that you have come up with and suggest that parents and carers use it too. Encourage them to laugh with their children when it is used so that the children feel it is clever and funny. Ask them to ignore any swearing at the same time so that the children do not find it attracts attention.

My turn, your turn

Group size
Two children, including the child that you are targeting.

What you need
A simple picture *Lotto* game comprising two boards and sets of cards, one for each child (you can make the game by using two boards ruled into nine sections, each with a picture of a familiar object, and making nine laminated cards for each board with identical pictures for matching one to one); bag or box to place the cards into.

What to do
Sit at a table so that the two children are seated opposite each other and you are between them, supporting the child that you are targeting.

Start by giving each child a board and the set of nine cards to match onto it. Encourage both children to talk about the pictures to hold their interest.

As a next step, place all the cards together in the bag and ask the child that you are targeting to draw one out. Help the children to scan their boards to see if they have that picture,

and encourage the child to pass it to their partner if necessary. Continue until all the cards have been drawn out of the bag.

Now repeat the game by drawing out the cards yourself, encouraging each child to tell you if it belongs to their board. Start by ensuring that the children have alternative turns, then set it up so that one might have to wait a little longer for their next card. Praise their patience and turn-taking.

At a later session, stay close by as the two children organize this game themselves. Ensure that each waits for their turn before pulling out a card from the bag, one card at a time.

Special support
If a child's attention is very short, complete the board partially so that there are only three or four more cards to add. Make it particularly fun to complete the task by blowing a party whistle or letting the child set off a 'Jack-in-the-box'.

Hold the children's attention by having several sets of boards and pictures so that each game is novel. Allow an unsure child to watch first.

Extension
Encourage older children to make *Lotto* boards and matching cards by cutting and sticking old Christmas cards or catalogues.

LEARNING OBJECTIVE FOR ALL THE CHILDREN
● to take turns when working as part of a group.

INDIVIDUAL BEHAVIOUR TARGET
● to take turns in a simple game with one other child.

LINKS WITH HOME
Lend the *Lotto* board and cards to the child to take home and ask parents to play with them.

Fair share

Group size
Three children, including the child that you are targeting.

What you need
Attractive card and coloured paper; washable felt-tipped pens; coloured glitter sticks or glitter glue pen; table.

What to do
Arrange the art materials on a table. You can link this activity to your present project, for example, making greetings cards, a fireworks frieze or an underwater collage. Encourage the children to sit down at the table. Sit near to the child that you are targeting. Show how the glitter sticks work and encourage the children to practise with different colours and effects. Now help them to choose card, pens and glitter for the creation of your choice, or simply for the pure pleasure of the process. Talk about the colours that they need before they start. Point out that they both need the same colours. How can they share fairly? Talk about taking turns, and show them how to ask rather than take.

Support the children as they work, praising and encouraging all attempts to ask and to pass the glitter pens and the felt-tipped pens between themselves.

Special support
Use an egg timer to support fair turn-taking in other activities. Help those children who find it hard to share by encouraging them to hand out the snacks and drinks at snack time and to give out the musical instruments at music time.

Provide a special holder for the pens to sit in on the table so that the children are not tempted to hoard them all. Praise each child for matching the pen back to a coloured slot in the holder when they have finished using it.

Extension
Encourage older children to think of different ways in which they can be helped to share fairly during the various activities on offer in your group.

LEARNING OBJECTIVE FOR ALL THE CHILDREN
● to work as part of a group, sharing fairly.

INDIVIDUAL BEHAVIOUR TARGET
● to share a glitter stick with two other children.

LINKS WITH HOME
Ask parents and carers to encourage their children to share out food or snacks at home. If they have brothers or sisters, the children can also be encouraged to share fairly together.

LEARNING OBJECTIVE FOR ALL THE CHILDREN
● to understand that people have different cultures and beliefs which need to be treated with respect.

INDIVIDUAL BEHAVIOUR TARGET
● to feel confident with new routines and new people.

LINKS WITH HOME
Ask parents and carers to help their children bring in food items and objects of relevance to your festival. Be specific about what they should look out for.

Knowing me, knowing you

Group size
All the children.

What you need
Props and celebratory food relevant to a celebration or festival of your choice.

What to do
Choose a current festival, for example, Chinese New Year, Hanukkah, Passover, Christmas, or even a special birthday celebration relevant to one particular culture. Read up about the way in which this festival is celebrated, for example, in the *Around the Year* series (Scholastic). Involve parents and carers or members of your local community to help you prepare and to join in on the occasion.

Get ready together for the celebration, using pictures and stories regularly to explain to the children what the festival is about and what happens during the celebrations. Encourage them to ask questions and find out more together. Build up to the occasion and enjoy your celebration together.

Special support
Involve your targeted child in all the stages of your preparation. Some children find it very difficult to cope with new events, and it helps them to understand in advance what is going to happen.

Others quickly become very excited. Prepare them with a specific job to do, such as handing out the cakes, so that they have somewhere to channel their energy and focus their attention.

Use an additional adult helper to support the child that you are targeting throughout the celebration. Withdraw together to somewhere quiet from time to time if the child needs to calm down. Return as soon as you feel that they are ready to.

Extension
Encourage older children to help you plan the occasion and to 'research' the festival through talking with visitors and going to the local library or resource centre with parents and carers or staff.

Minding myself

Group size
One child.

What you need
A clean and secure toilet area (provide steps and seat inserts if necessary); coloured food dye; glitter; liquid soap.

What to do
Decorate the area with colours, posters, flowers and accessories to make it homely. If a child has been slow at using the toilet independently, wait until you feel that they are ready – they need to be aware of when their bladder or bowels are full and they feel comfortable sitting on the toilet. Before they are ready to come out of nappies, make visits to the toilet area happy and familiar.

When you decide to 'give it a try', discuss this with the parents or carers. Suggest that you try removing the nappy during the nursery session and use trainer pants instead. Keep a note of any 'accidents' to help you judge when the best times are to encourage the child to try the toilet. Encourage the child to 'try' regularly, even if they cannot 'go', and praise all attempts. Keep an eye on the child who is so busy playing that they forget to go. Be aware of the signs indicating that the child needs to go to the toilet.

Calmly help the child finish what they are doing and chat together as you visit the toilet. Stay outside the door chatting as the child tries to 'go'. Help them remove and pull up clothing by providing just the amount of help necessary, no more. Deal with any 'accidents' calmly and discreetly, without making a fuss or giving the child too much attention.

If the child manages successfully, praise their efforts and encourage them to pull the chain. If your cistern allows for it, you will have placed a small amount of food colouring, soap liquid or glitter (or all three) in the cistern. Share your celebration with the surprise effect!

Special support
You need not use this technicolour approach for ever! Fade this out so that it only happens occasionally. Use shiny star stickers and charts to encourage success.

Extension
Show older children how to wash their hands properly and become fully independent.

LEARNING OBJECTIVE FOR ALL THE CHILDREN
● to manage their own personal hygiene.

INDIVIDUAL BEHAVIOUR TARGET
● to go to the toilet independently.

LINKS WITH HOME
Share progress on toilet training with parents and carers so that they can build on your successes and vice-versa.

LEARNING OBJECTIVE FOR ALL THE CHILDREN
● to work as part of a group, taking turns.

INDIVIDUAL BEHAVIOUR TARGETS
● to take turns within a small group of children
● to develop positive self-esteem.

King of the castle

Group size
Four children.

What you need
Nine building blocks (either large foam cubes or smaller wooden blocks); hard floor surface; four toy people or animals.

What to do
Gather the children in a circle and sit together on the floor. Place your targeted child next to you. Allow each child to choose a toy – to make it climb the tower that you are going to build together. Share the blocks out so that each child has three blocks.

Encourage the children to place one block at a time to make a tower, taking turns to build the next block. When the last block is placed carefully on top, encourage the child who placed it to put their toy on the top and make it dance as it chants 'I'm the king of the castle!'. Encourage the children to make the other toys dance on the ground and cheer.

Repeat the activity twice more, starting at a different point in the circle so that each child's toy has a turn to be 'king'. Praise the children for taking turns and make a fuss of the 'winner' each time.

Special support
Use distraction to keep any very active children from knocking the tower down. Keep chattering, give them the next block and toy to hold and direct their attention onto what is going on. Make the game as exciting as possible.

If you feel that the children in your group have a short attention span, start this activity with just two children and four bricks.

Extension
Encourage older children to co-operate in building castles for their toys to share.

LINKS WITH HOME
Send some small blocks home for a turn-taking building game. Ask parents and carers to praise their children for taking turns and for concentrating carefully when balancing the blocks.

COMMUNICATION, LANGUAGE AND LITERACY

This chapter has ten activities for encouraging all children to develop skills in this area. Ideas are given for children who may need particular support to concentrate and to feel successful.

Old MacDonald's book

LEARNING OBJECTIVE FOR ALL THE CHILDREN
● to link sounds to letters.

INDIVIDUAL BEHAVIOUR TARGETS
● to look and listen within a group;
● to join in with confidence.

Group size
Eight to twelve children.

What you need
Three stiff cardboard or ply cut-outs of the particular letters you are working on, such as 'm', 's' and 'b'.

What to do
Gather the children in a circle for this song. Place the letter shapes behind you for the moment. Teach the children this song, to the usual tune of 'Old MacDonald Had a Farm':

> Old MacDonald had a book, E – I – E – I – O!
> And in that book he had a 'mmmmm' (or 'ssss'), E – I – E – I – O!
> With a 'mmmmmmmmmm' here and a 'mmmmmmmmmm' there,
> Here a 'mmmmmmm', there a 'mmmmmmm', everywhere a 'mmmmmmm'
> Old MacDonald had a book, E – I – E – I – O!

As you introduce each new sound, pass the letter shape around the circle. Repeat for the other two letter shapes. Now place the three shapes in the centre of the circle. Invite any child who might find this task particularly difficult to pick one up and to show it to the rest of the group. Invite the children to tell you what it says. Ask the child holding it if they are correct (this way, the child with difficulties is not experiencing failure). Sing the verse which goes with the letter as the child shows it to everyone around the circle.

Special support
Sit an additional helper near to any child who is going to find it hard to behave and to concentrate.

Continue the activity later on a one-to-one basis, seeing if the child can link the sounds to the letter shapes. Gradually introduce more children and a larger selection of letters to the song in future sessions.

Extension
Invite older children to suggest animals and sounds for your song.

LINKS WITH HOME
Give the child a letter shape to take home and invite the parents or carers to help them find three things which begin with that sound. Ask the child to tell you what they found the next day.

Libraries

Group size
All the children, two or three at a time for the 'visit'.

What you need
Low bookshelves; assortment of books (preferably unfamiliar ones, perhaps on library loan); low desk; chair; rubber stamp and ink pad; selection of pencils; 'Post-it' notes; cushioned area for looking at books; additional adult helpers or older children to share books with children who ask them.

What to do
Set up your usual book corner to represent a library. Have a selection of books easily accessible on the shelves. Prominently display any books that the children have not seen before to attract their attention. Set up a desk and chair for the 'librarian'. Show the librarian how to stamp the 'Post-it' slip and stick it into the front of the book. Encourage them to write in a number to represent the date. Talk to the group about how libraries work as you set up this activity together. Ask your additional helpers to be on hand to talk through and share the books if the children invite them to.

Encourage the child that you are targeting to be the librarian. Invite other children to visit the library, choose a book, and enjoy taking it to the cushions to 'read' or share with an adult. As the librarian stamps the slip, encourage the children to say 'please' and 'thank you' appropriately. Comment on what a polite and helpful library this is.

Special support
Make sure that you stay close to encourage appropriate behaviour and language. Model the 'please' and 'thank you' each time if it is not spoken spontaneously.

Extension
Invite older children to select and arrange the books. Organize library 'talks' where they tell the other children why they like certain books.

Are you receiving me?

Group size
One child at a time for about five minutes each.

What to do
Invite the children (including the child that you are targeting) to take it in turns to be your messenger. Explain that you need them to help you tell people things. Gain the messenger's attention with their name and give them a simple message. Ask them to repeat it to you and watch to make sure that they follow it through correctly, helping if you need to. You might ask them to tell a colleague that coffee is ready, or to tell another child that they can paint now. You could also ask them to tell another child that their model is really good; thank a child for sharing the play dough or tell everyone that it will soon be tidy-up time. Gear the length of the message to the level of understanding of each child, emphasizing the key words.

Praise each child warmly for their help and offer a special 'helper' sticker at the end of their turn.

Special support
Help children with limited attention by getting down to their level before speaking, saying their name and offering a light touch to hold their attention. Gain full eye contact, however fleeting, before speaking. Keep the message simple and ask them to say it back – for example, 'coffee time!'.

Keep the turns very short for children with behaviour and attention difficulties, rewarding after one message at first.

Offer a reassuring hand to a child who is particularly shy, and go with them to relay the message. If necessary, say it for them and ask them to nod if it was correct.

Extension
Older children will be able to cope with more complex messages and may be sent (in pairs), for example, to another classroom.

LEARNING OBJECTIVE FOR ALL THE CHILDREN
● to sustain attentive listening, responding to what they have heard with relevant actions.

INDIVIDUAL BEHAVIOUR TARGET
● to give eye contact when spoken to.

LINKS WITH HOME
Encourage parents and carers to use the same methods to gain their children's full attention and eye contact before relaying simple messages and instructions. If the child is non-compliant, they can add a simple '1-2-3' count, guiding the child through the action if they do not respond. Again, they need to praise all compliance, even if the child was helped.

Traffic signals

Group size
Four to six children.

What you need
A hard playground area; disc of card (35cm in diameter); dowelling (approximately 1m); sticky tape; paint; two pieces of card (30cm x 20 cm); chalk; your usual cars, bikes and tractors.

What to do
Make a traffic signal by attaching the card disc to the end of the piece of dowelling using sticky tape. One side should be green with the word 'GO', and the other side should be red with the word 'STOP'. Then take your two pieces of card and on one write 'GO' and on the other write 'STOP'.

Use the chalk to set up a circular road system in your playground area. Define clearly where the roads are and make them wide enough for two vehicles to pass with plenty of room. Start off by being the 'police officer'. Stand at one point of the road and encourage the children to stop when they see the red sign and go when they see the green one. Then invite them to read the words. When they are used to this activity, swap the traffic signal for the two cards, using these to tell the children to stop or to go. Make sure that there are several children together so that they can copy one another if necessary.

Finally, encourage the children to take it in turns to be the police officer. Explain that you are the traffic controller and that the police officer should show the sign that you ask them to. Step to one side and hold up the 'stop' card or the 'go' card for your 'police officer' to read, and encourage them to change the traffic signal accordingly.

Special support
Children with low self-esteem will enjoy being the police officer. Stay close by to encourage and support them.

If the children become wild, step in as traffic controller and explain that they will need to park until you make their engines slower. Pretend to tune the engine and send them on their way when they have settled a little. Praise the children regularly for staying on the track.

Extension
Encourage older children to use chalks to design road lay-outs for everyone to enjoy.

LEARNING OBJECTIVE FOR ALL THE CHILDREN
● to take turns in a conversation.

INDIVIDUAL BEHAVIOUR TARGET
● to leave gaps for the speaker to respond when speaking.

LINKS WITH HOME
Tell parents and carers that you have been talking about using the telephone and ask them to find an opportunity for their children to telephone a favourite relative or friend.

Telephone talk

Group size
Two children at a time.

What you need
A toy telephone for each child; curtain screen; tables; chairs.

What to do
Set up the telephones, screen, tables and chairs to look like two office spaces. If you have the chance to use an internal telephone system with real telephones, this works even better (although if you are using two separate rooms, you will need an adult helper in each room).

Encourage the child that you are targeting to come to the telephone. Explain that they can telephone a friend. Who would they like to talk to? Call the chosen friend to the other telephone. Stay by any child who needs help to encourage them to talk and to listen, by suggesting things to say such as: 'Hello'; 'Who is it?'; How are you?'; 'What are you doing today?'; 'Goodbye' and so on. Praise them for speaking clearly and for listening well. Now invite the child who was telephoned to choose a new friend to telephone and continue the activity in this way.

Special support
Some children talk non-stop and do not wait for gaps for the listener to reply. Encourage listening as well as speaking by holding and removing the handset after each phrase.

Keep conversations short for children with short attention spans, gradually building them up. Find real purposes for the calls, for example, to ask Sharif to play on the train.

Extension
Talk about making real telephone calls. Ask older children to phone a simple message to the office or to home with your help. Talk about the emergency services. When do people make 999 calls? Why is it important not to make 999 calls unless you need help?

Big voice, little voice

Group size
All the children.

What you need
The rhyme on the photociaple sheet on page 88; additional helper or support assistant to sit next to any child that you are targeting.

What to do
Sit down together in a circle. You might choose to use this activity as part of your regular circle time or music time. Teach the rhyme to the children. As you chant the first verse, make two fingers into a beater and tap them lightly against the open palm of your other hand. Take it slowly. As you chant the second verse, clap your hands loudly to the rhythm. Praise the children for using their little voices and then their big voices. When would we use little voices? (for example, when someone is sleeping; when talking to a little baby; when trying not to disturb somebody and so on). When would

we use big voices? (for example, when calling to somebody in the playing field; when shouting for help and so on).

Follow up this activity by praising the children for using their little voices when other children are busy playing.

Special support
If a child persistently shouts, have a practice at the beginning of the session using their big voice and then their little voice. Spot the child using their little voice later and praise them as often as you notice.

If a child has only found their little voice, tape-record this and play it back to them amplified so that they can hear their big voice too. Practise big voices using puppets.

Extension
Think of other rhymes and chants where you can use big voices and little voices.

LEARNING OBJECTIVES FOR ALL THE CHILDREN
● to explore and experiment with sounds, words and texts
● to speak clearly and audibly with confidence and control.

INDIVIDUAL BEHAVIOUR TARGETS
● to control the volume of the voice
● to develop positive self-esteem.

LINKS WITH HOME
Give each child a copy of the photocopiable sheet on page 88 to take home. Ask parents and carers to remind their children to find their little voices when others are trying to sleep.

LEARNING OBJECTIVE FOR ALL THE CHILDREN
● to extend their vocabulary, exploring the meanings of new words.

INDIVIDUAL BEHAVIOUR TARGETS
● to develop an understanding of the words 'kind' and 'gentle'
● to link words with actions.

Kind and gentle

Group size
Three or four children.

What you need
A glove puppet for each child and one for yourself (you can make these out of socks with button eyes if you need to).

What to do
Sit down together on the carpet. Give the puppet who is being kind to the child that you are targeting. Keep the puppet who is being naughty yourself. Give out the rest of the puppets, one to each child.
Suggest that the puppets play together. Sing a song as you make them dance. Play 'Catch' as you make them fly through the air. Suddenly the 'naughty' puppet decides to fight (gently) another puppet. Share the problem together: what should happen now? Perhaps the other puppets should tell it to stop? Perhaps the 'kind' puppet could make the 'hurt' puppet feel better. What could the kind puppet do?

Encourage the kind puppet to show the naughty puppet how to play gently and how to dance gently. Talk about what it means to be 'kind' and 'gentle' and help the children to think of examples. Praise the kind puppet for helping.

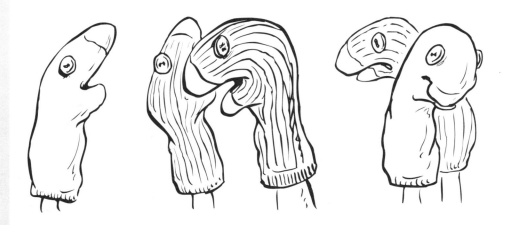

Special support
Stay close to any child who is likely to develop the game aggressively or to take control. Allow them to take control in a 'kind' way and praise them for doing so.

Give more attention to the kind and gentle puppets than to the naughty ones.

Follow up by showing the children how to behave in kind and gentle ways throughout the session.

Extension
Encourage older children to look after the new starters and/or the younger children.

LINKS WITH HOME
Tell parents and carers that you have all been talking about being 'kind' and 'gentle'. Ask them to help their children find one kind thing to do that day at home.

COMMUNICATION, LANGUAGE & LITERACY

LEARNING OBJECTIVE FOR ALL THE CHILDREN
- to use talk to organize, sequence and clarify thinking, ideas, feelings and events.

INDIVIDUAL BEHAVIOUR TARGET
- to develop confidence when speaking with a familiar adult.

LINKS WITH HOME
Keep the parents or carers in touch with their child's worries and concerns, however trivial they might seem. If you have real concerns about Child Protection, follow your usual procedures.

Special time

Group size
All the children can be involved, one at a time when needed.

What you need
Floor space; cushions; soft music; bubble light; additional adult helper.

What to do
Set up a 'quiet area' with cushions, lighting and music. Ideally, this should be on the edge of the play area and not isolated from it. Each child should have a named key worker with whom they can become familiar over a number of sessions. The key worker of the child that you are targeting should also be available to offer particular support to that child.

Whenever a child is particularly upset or angry, withdraw to your quiet area. Avoid eye contact and words as you gently withdraw together and settle the child on the cushions. Stay nearby as the child calms down. If the child comes out, calmly return them. Once they are calm and settled, begin to talk together. Ask them questions such as, 'What went wrong?', 'What happened?', 'I can see that you are sad/cross today, would it help to talk about it?', 'How can we say "sorry"?', 'Shall I help you?' and so on.

Special support
Sometimes children are frightened after a violent tantrum. As soon as they are calm, give them plenty of attention, reassurance and comfort. Help them to put things right if there has been a fight, stating the rules again calmly and firmly and listening to what they have to say.

If the children are making themselves cry, offer a precious little bottle to collect the tears to show Mum. Sometimes, the tears dry up with the effort!

Do not attempt to talk to or reason with a child who is highly upset – they need to calm down before they can cope with your input.

Extension
Offer your quiet area to any child who wants time to talk with their key worker, sharing good news as well as difficulties.

LEARNING OBJECTIVE FOR ALL THE CHILDREN

● to hear and say initial and final sounds in words.

INDIVIDUAL BEHAVIOUR TARGET

● to pay attention when listening.

I hear with my little ear

Group size
Three to four children.

What you need
A tray with six familiar objects or picture cards which have regular consonant-vowel-consonant labels, such as a jug, cat, bed, top, van and fox (try to select objects so that each has a word ending or a word beginning unique to itself without any overlap); additional adult helper to support any targeted child.

What to do
Gather the children in a circle and sit together on the floor. Introduce the tray of objects and pass each one around as you name it together. Explain that you are going to play a guessing game. Say:

I hear with my little ear
Something which starts with ('f')...

Put in the beginning letter sound of one of the objects. At first, the children will find this extremely difficult, so repeat the 'f' sound as you say each object's name, searching together for a match. Once they have found the correct object, repeat that rhyme once more so that they can all answer immediately.

Once the children can manage this, and probably at a later session, try:

I hear with my little ear
Something which ends with ('d')...

Again, support and help the children as they find a match.

Special support
Start with only two objects that have very different sounds. Invite an additional helper to repeat and emphasize the sound for the child that you are targeting and to provide them with one-to-one support.

Invite the child to whisper to you which object you should choose next, in order to keep their interest.

Extension
Extend this activity by introducing words that have a variety of middle sounds but still have clear beginning sounds and end sounds.

LINKS WITH HOME
Encourage the children and their parents or carers to play this game at home.

LEARNING OBJECTIVE FOR ALL THE CHILDREN
● to tell a narrative in the correct sequence.

INDIVIDUAL BEHAVIOUR TARGET
● to develop the confidence to speak in a small group.

One fine day...

Group size
Four to six children.

..dog and I hid behind the...

...wall

What to do
Sit down together in a circle. Sit the child that you are targeting next to you on your left. Tell the children that they are going to make up a story together all about a funny walk.

Start the story yourself: '*One fine day, I went for a walk. I saw a...*'. Invite the child on your left to choose a word to go in. Now turn to the next child in the circle and build the story up: '*One fine day, I went for a walk. I saw a... (pause for that child to say the word chosen by the first child) and I said...*' – invite that child to fill in the blank. Build the story up in this way so that each child has to remember more words. Your story might end up something like this: '*One fine day, I went for a walk. I saw a... and I said... so I went to the... and I had a big... Then I went home to find my... and I hid behind the...*'.

Encourage the other children to help if a child needs it.

Special support
Keep turning to the child on your left to ask 'Was that right? Can you remember too?'.

Keep the group small and start with two or three children if you feel you need to.

Offer some choices if the child feels unable to think of one.

Praise the children for sitting still and keep the activity short enough to end on a successful note.

Extension
Use this activity to encourage older children to develop more complex story sequences.

LINKS WITH HOME
Ask the parents or carers to spend a few moments at bedtime talking about their child's day and what happened in it.

MATHEMATICAL DEVELOPMENT

This chapter will help all the children's mathematical development but should also provide motivation for those who find it hard to behave and to settle. There are ideas for encouraging children to feel successful in their learning through early number work.

LEARNING OBJECTIVE FOR ALL THE CHILDREN
● to recognize numerals.

INDIVIDUAL BEHAVIOUR TARGET
● to watch carefully and identify the numerals '1' and '2'.

Spin the plate

Group size
Two children at a time.

What you need
A round plastic picnic plate; sticky label to cover the centre of the plate; felt-tipped pen, twelve carpet squares.

What to do
Stick a label over the centre of each side of the plate and write on one side a large '1', and on the other a '2' (or alternatively write directly onto the plate). Arrange the carpet squares in a circle on a carpet so that there is one child's pace between the centres from one square to the other, and so that they do not slide.

Invite two children (including the child that you are targeting) to join you for a game. Show them the plate and say the numbers out loud together. Hold one side of the plate to face both children and encourage them to call out the name of the number (one child's answer will therefore help the other's). Now show the children how you can spin the plate and see which number lands uppermost. Try again several times, inviting the children to call out the number.

Now position yourself on one of the carpet squares and spin the plate. Count out loud as you take 'one' or 'two' steps to reach the next square.

Finally, start the children at opposite sides of the circle, each standing on a carpet square. Invite them to take it in turns to spin the plate as the other child takes the matching number of steps around the circle.

Special support
If a child finds it difficult to control their own behaviour, they might need an adult to hold their hand, help them take the strides and stay in position. The support should aim to be motivating and encouraging.

If necessary, involve a third child in spinning the plate so that you can hold one of the children's hands and provide encouragement.

Extension
Use higher numerals for older children, and perhaps choose from several plates with different numerals each time.

LINKS WITH HOME
Ask parents and carers to help their children count as they walk up steps or stairs, taking one step for each count.

Dotty dominoes

Group size
Two children at a time.

What you need
The minibeast pictures cut out from the photocopiable sheet on page 89; card (large enough to glue two of the minibeast pictures on, side by side); scissors (adult use); glue; laminator.

What to do
Use the template on page 89 to make a set of 15 dominoes – take six photocopies to provide enough of each number. Cut each 'set' of minibeasts out and glue them onto one end of the pre-cut card to make dominoes. Do not include sections with no minibeasts on; in this way you will end up with a small set of 15 dominoes. Laminate them to make them strong and attractive to use.

Start by working individually with the child that you are targeting. Sit down at a table and spread the dominoes out, picture side up, matching them together to make a chain, one minibeast next to one minibeast, five minibeasts next to five and so on. Count them out as you match the pictures.

Once the child understands the game, invite one other child to join in. Spread all the dominoes out and encourage the children to take it in turns to choose a domino to match onto the one before. This simpler version of the game is non-competitive and the aim is to make the chain as long as possible.

Special support
Praise the child for waiting for their turn. Invite the children to help one another to find a domino or count the minibeasts.

If the children you are working with have limited concentration spans, use a smaller set of dominoes, involving sets of one, two and three minibeasts. End on a successful note.

Extension
Build up to using proper dominoes and counting larger sets.

Alternatively, design your own set, this time ensuring that the creatures are randomly arranged so that the children have to count them more carefully.

LEARNING OBJECTIVE FOR ALL THE CHILDREN
● to count reliably up to five.

INDIVIDUAL BEHAVIOUR TARGET
● to take turns with one other child.

LINKS WITH HOME
Lend your set of dominoes to parents and carers for them to play with their children at home.

Two little hands

Group size
Eight to ten children.

What to do
Gather the children in a circle, kneeling on the floor and facing one another across the circle. This activity might form part of your regular circle time or music time. Practise this rhyme together:

> Two little hands to wave to my friends
> HEL-LO! HEL-LO!
> Two little hands to clap when I'm happy
> ONE, TWO! ONE, TWO!
> Two little hands to walk up the staircase
> ONE, TWO! ONE, TWO!
> Two little hands to dry away my tear drops
> BOO, HOO! BOO, HOO!
>
> *Hannah Mortimer*

Wave 'hello' for the first phrase and clap your hands together in rhythm as you chant 'ONE, TWO' in the second phrase. 'March' your hands on the carpet for a beat of 'ONE, TWO' in the third and exaggerate the loud crying and sobbing in the last line to keep it fun.

Follow this up with a one-two rhythm chant such as 'Cobbler, Cobbler, Mend my Shoe' (Traditional). Have everyone chanting 'one-two, one-two' as they march their hands on the floor before and after the chant.

Special support
If necessary, kneel behind any child who finds it hard to settle, helping them to do the actions and maintaining their interest. Use the last line to capture their motivation and share the fun of it together.

If a child is at the very early stages of settling, allow them to stay outside the circle, but praise them for looking when you all burst into 'crocodile tears' at the end.

Extension
Encourage the children to join you in playing a marching game where you all march to a 'one-two' chant and try to keep the beat (perhaps have an adult helper playing the beat on a drum).

LEARNING OBJECTIVE FOR ALL THE CHILDREN

● to use everyday words to describe position.

INDIVIDUAL BEHAVIOUR TARGETS

● to feel comfortable within their own space

● to allow a familiar adult into their play.

LINKS WITH HOME
Encourage parents and carers to help their children make simple houses out of shoeboxes, glue and snippets of material. Ask them to play a game – challenging the child to place a toy person 'in', 'on', 'under', 'outside' and 'inside' the box.

My space

Group size
Two or three children at a time.

What you need
Two or three large cardboard boxes from a supermarket; large scissors (adult use); sticky tape; thick felt-tipped marker pen.

What to do
Encourage two or three children (including the child that you are targeting) to help you build a house. Show the children your boxes and involve them as you make them into 'houses'. Ask each child where they would like the windows to be and where to cut the door. Use the sticky

tape to reinforce the boxes. Use the marker pen to add details. Follow up any other suggestions that the children might have – props for the inside, curtains for the windows and so on. Place the houses together to make a 'street' or 'estate'.

Encourage the children to enjoy their own spaces and to invite one another in, in a friendly manner. Show them how to knock at a door or how to ask one another around. Use your commentary to emphasize position words such as 'inside', 'outside', 'under' the table, 'over' the roof and so on. Be sure to respect the children's spaces, and always ask permission to join them.

At the end of the game, find a way of closing it, for example, by 'going away on holiday' or 'giving their house to someone else to play in' because they are going to be too busy.

Special support
Children whose self-esteem is low will feel boosted by the part they play in the house design. Allow them their own space, staying close by to support if needed.

Children who quickly become emotional or aggressive may find it helpful to have their own private space to withdraw to. Use it to help them 'cool down' or stay calm.

Extension
Sit down with paper and pencil and design your houses in advance. Afterwards, review together how well the design matched the plan.

Three wobbly jellyfish

Group size
Ten to twelve children.

What you need
A large tambourine.

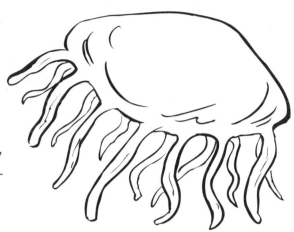

What to do
Sit on the floor in a circle. Tell the children that you are going to play some shaking music. When they hear it, they are to shake – shake their arms, shake their toes, shake their bodies all over! When the music stops, they should stop too. Are they listening? Are they looking? Move around the circle as you shake the tambourine loudly, encouraging the children to shake. Then beat the tambourine once loudly, stopping absolutely still. Praise the children by name for looking and listening. Repeat three or four times, encouraging laughter and giggles as you shake, and scanning all the children's faces when you have stopped.

Move on straight away to a shaking song. Ask the children to show you three fingers and count them all together 'one, two, three'. The following words can be sung to the tune of 'Three Blind Mice':

> Three green jellyfish, three green jellyfish
> Sat upon a rock, sat upon a rock
> The first one felt like a swim, you know,
> And slithered away to the sea, you know,
> And left the rest on their own-i-o,
> Just two green jellyfish.
>
> *Hannah Mortimer*

Wobble all over for the word 'jellyfish'. Raise your hands in the air and wobble them down all the way to the sea for the 'slithering'. Repeat two more times until there are no jellyfish left on the rock. Stop to count fingers each time.

Special support
Praise the children for looking and listening so well. Use a child's name from time to time to say, '(Ellie), you *are* listening well'.

Give a very active child the tambourine to shake each time you say the word 'jellyfish'.

Extension
Encourage the children to help you make jellyfish with long tissue tentacles and act out the verses together, shaking these at the same time.

LEARNING OBJECTIVES FOR ALL THE CHILDREN
● to count reliably up to 10 everyday objects
● to talk about, recognize and re-create simple patterns.

INDIVIDUAL BEHAVIOUR TARGET
● to develop confidence in one-to-one correspondence.

LINKS WITH HOME
Ask parents and carers to challenge their children to show them 'five' or 'ten' fingers and then to touch each fingertip as they count them together.

Long line

Group size
Two children at a time.

What you need
Large building bricks, ten of one shape (perhaps oblong) and ten of another (perhaps square). Alternatively, use ten bricks of one colour and ten of another.

What to do
Arrange the bricks into two piles on the floor – five oblong and five square in each set. Invite two children (including the child that you are targeting) to join you for a copying game.

Start by having one pile of bricks yourself and giving the other pile to the two children. Place one of your bricks down and invite the children to place an identical one from their own pile just beside it. Continue to build up your tower, brick by brick, as the children select matching bricks from their own pile to make an identical tower. Compare the patterns. Count the bricks by touching each one in sequence and counting out loud. Are they the same?

Now start again, inviting the child that you are targeting to build another tower and the other child to copy it right beside it. Stop to compare patterns and count bricks.

Finally, encourage the first child to copy the pattern made by the other.

Special support
Use your presence to encourage and support, using a gentle hand-over-hand support to count the numbers.

If the child's attention span is very short, touch the bricks when you are counting and count alternate numbers, encouraging the child to come in with even ones.

Extension
Dip into your brick box to make more complex patterns with higher numbers of bricks. Try encouraging the children to copy a tower of bricks placed apart rather than side by side so that direct comparisons are more difficult.

Body shapes

Group size
Three children and their parents or carers.

What you need
A roll of lining paper; washable felt-tipped pens; additional helper.

What to do
Explain to parents and carers that you would welcome their help in an activity to teach the children about 'taller' and 'shorter'. Tell them that the children are going to trace around them. Would they be willing for their children to draw them? (They might appreciate a warning so that they can wear appropriate clothing or opt out if they would prefer.)

Make a quiet carpeted area available. Invite the children and their parents or carers to gather around. Tear off a strip of paper and lie down on it, inviting your helper to trace around your body shape. Now do the same to your helper. When the children understand what is happening, invite their carers in turn to lie down on a sheet of paper. Help each child to choose a pen and draw approximately around the outline. When they have finished, encourage the carer to help their child lie inside the outline they have traced and have their own outline traced there. Why is one smaller than the other? Who is taller? Who is shorter?

Special support
This activity is used as part of relationship play therapy and is a way of gradually helping carers and children to tolerate more physical contact and feel at ease with each other.

Use the shape of one outline surrounding the other to talk with the children about caring and looking after each other.

If any of the children find this activity threatening, start by drawing hand shapes first and then try foot shapes.

Extension
Encourage the children to compare one another's sizes and use the appropriate vocabulary to describe 'taller' and 'shorter'.

LEARNING OBJECTIVE FOR ALL THE CHILDREN
● to use language such as 'taller' and 'shorter' when comparing sizes.

INDIVIDUAL BEHAVIOUR TARGETS
● to develop confidence in physical contact
● to share an activity in a small group.

LINKS WITH HOME
Send the body traces home and ask parents and carers to spend time adding faces and expressions to them with their children.

LEARNING OBJECTIVE FOR ALL THE CHILDREN
● to begin to relate addition to combining objects.

INDIVIDUAL BEHAVIOUR TARGETS
● to interact appropriately with other children
● to develop positive self-esteem.

How old are you?

Group size
One child to help you prepare; all the children to complete the activity.

What you need
A piece of card for each child (approximately 10cm x 10cm); felt-tipped pens; large sheet of sugar paper or lining paper.

What to do
Invite the child that you are targeting to help you prepare, asking them to be your helper as you get ready for a game about ages. How old is your helper? Write the number down on a card together. If they are able, they can write it independently, otherwise they can copy, trace over, or you can provide them with hand-over-hand support.

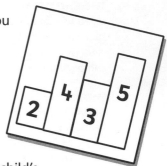

Now explain that you need to find out every child's age in the group. Suggest children by name and send your targeted child to ask how old they are. Model how to say 'excuse me' first and 'thank you' afterwards. If you can stand back to allow them to do it themselves, that is excellent. Otherwise, go with them for support. Each time, return to your table to write the number down on a card.

When you have all the ages written down, bring the cards out at circle time and spread them number side up on the floor. Invite each child to come and choose their age number and stick it onto a bar chart drawn on the large sheet of paper.

Special support
Praise the child that you are targeting in front of the other children for writing all the numbers.

Extension
Discuss the bar chart together and decide what information it gives you. Look for other ways of recording ages and birthdays.

LINKS WITH HOME
Send some blank cards home for the children to practise writing numbers. Ask parents and carers to help them spot numbers on packaging and instructions around the house and copy them.

LEARNING OBJECTIVE FOR ALL THE CHILDREN
● to say and use number names in order in familiar contexts.

INDIVIDUAL BEHAVIOUR TARGET
● to begin to control impulsive behaviour.

One, two, three... GO!

Group size
All the children, at different times of day.

What you need
The photocopiable sheet on page 90.

What to do
Use this activity to make sure that the children are looking and listening, to make it more fun for them to do what you ask, and to train them to be compliant when you really mean something.

First, teach the children a signal which you will use when you really need to speak with them all. An idea is to call out 'touch your heads' or 'hands up high' – this keeps hands from being otherwise occupied for a moment or two. Another idea is to use a special sound such as a tambourine or the toot of a trumpet. Alternatively, depending on the ages and stages of the children, simply touch a child on the shoulder and hold their hands up high. That child touches the other children near them lightly on the shoulder and also puts their hands up. This quiet behaviour gradually spreads until everyone is holding up hands expectantly. Jenny Mosley has very useful ideas for this kind of attention (see page 95). When you have all the children's attention, tell them what you need to say (for example, 'Time to tidy up, please'), then encourage everyone to join in as you say, 'One, two, three... GO!'.

When you are particularly pleased with a child's behaviour, use the certificate on the photocopiable sheet on page 90. Invite the child to add a smiley face as you write in the behaviour you are celebrating today.

Special support
When you need to tell an individual child something important, go down to the same level as them, gain their eye contact, say their name, give a simple instruction, then say 'one, two, three...' as you wait for them to comply. If they do not comply, gently lead them through the action you have requested and thank them for doing so.

Extension
Challenge the children to do difficult jobs (such as putting all the cars away) after saying 'one, two, three... GO!'. Time them with a stopwatch and keep it fun and encouraging.

LINKS WITH HOME
● Encourage the child to take home the celebration certificate and share it with their family.
● Suggest that parents and carers use the 'one, two, three' warnings when they need their children to do as they say. These work best if they are kept for those events where it really matters and where carers follow through with support every single time.

LEARNING OBJECTIVE FOR ALL THE CHILDREN
● to use the vocabulary involved in adding and subtracting.

INDIVIDUAL BEHAVIOUR TARGET
● to co-operate in a group task.

Five little millipedes

Group size
Five children.

What you need
A picture of a millipede; five A4 cards; felt-tipped pens; scissors (adult use); lengths of carpet wool; glue; glue sticks; table.

What to do
Arrange the materials on a table and sit around it. Keep the child that you are targeting next to you if necessary. Show the children your picture of a millipede and admire its legs! Draw a millipede on each card and cut it out. Invite each child to take one of your millipedes and add wool 'legs' around its perimeter using the glue. Add eyes and a smile using the felt-tipped pens. Place the millipedes on one side to dry.

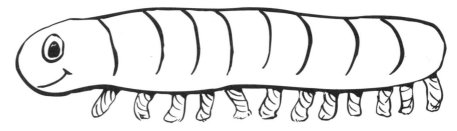

Now sit in a circle to sing this song, to the tune of the first two lines of 'Twinkle, Twinkle, Little Star' (Traditional):

> Five little millipedes went for a run
> Two flipped over and then there were…
>
> *Hannah Mortimer*

Each time, stop to encourage a child to flip or unflip the millipede(s), and ask everyone to count together to see how many are left. Vary the song by making some 'flip back' as well as 'flip over' and using different numbers each time – this makes it unpredictable so that the children have to re-count each time.

LINKS WITH HOME
Encourage parents and carers to practise the rhyme below with their children before bedtime:

> One, two, three, four, five; once I caught a fish alive
> Six, seven, eight, nine, ten; then I let it go again.
> Why did you let it go? Because it bit my finger so!
> Which finger did it bite? This little finger on my right!
>
> *Traditional*

Special support
Give an active child a regular job to do by flipping the millipede(s) or counting out. Keep the action rhyme simple (by flipping one at a time) if you think the child is going to find it threatening.

Praise the child regularly for joining in, looking and listening.

Extension
Ask older children to make an estimate of how many there are left before they count them.

KNOWLEDGE AND UNDERSTANDING OF THE WORLD

These activities are designed for all children in their knowledge and understanding of the world. There are also ideas for developing the confidence and self-esteem of children with difficulties.

LEARNING OBJECTIVE FOR ALL THE CHILDREN
● to observe, find out about and identify features in the place they live.

INDIVIDUAL BEHAVIOUR TARGET
● to say 'please' and 'thank you' when appropriate.

At your service

Group size
All the children, at different times.

What you need
Old greetings cards; scissors; writing materials; stickers to act as stamps; rubber stamps and ink pads; post-box made out of a cardboard box; postperson's bag and hat; real one-pence coins; low tables; chairs.

What to do
Set up your post-office area with one table for the server and others for the customers to write at. Encourage the child that you are targeting to take first turn as the postmaster or postmistress. Show them how to sit behind the desk and let them practise with the rubber stamps and ink pads. Make postcards together to 'sell' by cutting up old greetings cards. Prepare a tray of stickers to act as stamps.

Encourage your customers to call into the post office. Let them choose a postcard and ask to buy it, saying 'please'. When they hand over a one-pence coin, ask the postmaster or postmistress to say 'thank you'. Encourage the customer to sit at the table and 'write' a letter. Ask them which friend in the group the postcard should go to. Write the name on for them. Encourage them to 'buy' a stamp from the counter, and show them where to post the card. As the game progresses, encourage the child behind the counter to take on these helping roles themselves.

After a while, close the post office and help the child to become a postperson. Empty the post-box together and deliver all the cards using the post bag. Encourage and model 'thank you' again.

Now let other children take over and encourage the child that you are targeting to be a customer.

Special support
Show the child how they can help their 'customers' at the beginning of the game, then stand back when you are able. If you hear the child say 'please' and 'thank you' spontaneously, comment on how helpful the post office is today.

Extension
Encourage older children to write some words and add or copy the names onto the postcards.

LINKS WITH HOME
Send 'real' postcards to the children at their homes and ask parents and carers to help them read them.

My story

Group size
All the children, one or two at a time.

What you need
A scrapbook made of coloured sugar paper; sheets of drawing paper; scissors; removable latex glue; crayons; washable felt-tipped pens; some photographs and information from the children's homes.

What to do
Talk with the children's parents and carers first. Explain that you are going to be making a life story book for each child and that it would be helpful if they could let you borrow any photographs.

Work with one or two children at a time. Start the first page with the child's self-portrait. Ask the child what title they would like and write it in for them. Move onto pages about each of their family members, their home, when they were a baby and a toddler, what they like doing, and favourite memories.

Be flexible and allow the child to develop the book as they would like, depending on the materials and information you have available. If no photographs were sent in, talk with the child, do drawings together and mount these in the book instead. Make the books over several sessions.

Special support
Life story books are especially helpful for children who have had confused upbringings and need to make sense of the people and places in their lives. These children tend to reach for their books when they need an excuse to talk about their lives.

If a child is looked after by the local authority, find time to talk to the social worker or foster parents first so that this valuable work will fit in with their work with a child who has emotional needs. For such children, try to make a permanent record which they can keep with them and add to in any further placements.

Extension
Spend time talking about the past, the present and the future and help the children to sequence the events in their lives.

LEARNING OBJECTIVE FOR ALL THE CHILDREN
● to find out about past and present events in their own lives.

INDIVIDUAL BEHAVIOUR TARGET
● to develop confidence in talking about themselves.

LINKS WITH HOME
Use the photocopiable sheet on page 91 to gather information. Make time to talk with parents and carers first, particularly if they need to tell you about special circumstances. Find appropriate ways of gathering information from families who may not read English.

LEARNING OBJECTIVE FOR ALL THE CHILDREN
● to find out about present events in their setting.

INDIVIDUAL BEHAVIOUR TARGETS
● to link time of day with familiar routines
● to sequence events and predict what will happen next
● to feel settled and confident in a familiar routine.

Timetable

Group size
Four or five children.

What you need
A clock-face made of plastic or card with movable hands; up to twenty pieces of card (10cm x 10cm); pens; glue; strip of card 30cm wide and as long as you need it.

What to do
Sit down with the children, including the child that you are targeting. Talk about your nursery or playgroup session. What happens? Help the children put the events into a time sequence, for example, arriving; group time; play; drinks time; outside time; circle time; going home. What you decide on will depend on your setting and what kind of a routine you have. Ask the children to give you ideas so that you can represent each of these events on a piece of card – for example, a child taking off their coat to represent arriving; a child drinking and so on. Work together as you arrange your cards in time sequence on the table.

Now ask the children if they have any idea what time of day each event happens (you will need to help them here). Show them how to make the time on the clock-face and ask them to tell you what time it says. Help them to copy a clock-face onto a card for each of the different times of events that happen in your session.

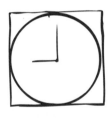

"At 9 o'clock we arrive."

"At half past 9 we have group time."

"At 11 o'clock we have drinks."

Now mount the cards on the strip of card to make a timetable, with each event sitting beside its corresponding clock-face. Mount it on the wall and show everybody at circle time.

Special support
Frequently refer to your timetable so that the child that you are targeting can understand what will happen next and when.

Extension
Encourage the children to draw their own pictures of routine events onto the cards.

LINKS WITH HOME
Make a simple pictorial timetable for the child that you are targeting to take home so that the parents or carers can talk with them about their session.

LEARNING OBJECTIVE FOR ALL THE CHILDREN
● to ask questions about why things happen and how things work.

INDIVIDUAL BEHAVIOUR TARGETS
● to think about caring
● to develop confidence in the presence of a nursery visitor.

LINKS WITH HOME
Link the activity to any pets that the child you are targeting might have. Look for good examples of caring so that you can praise them for looking after their pet so well. Ask the parents or carers to look for opportunities of letting their child care for a pet and to praise gentleness and caring behaviour.

At the vet's

Group size
All the children for the visit; three to four at a time for the play corner.

What you need
A local veterinary surgery that can be visited (or a local vet willing to visit you); any veterinary equipment which is safe for the children to handle and play with; books and stories about animals and vets; toy medical kit and other 'props' to make a vet's surgery; paper and pencils for recording 'prescriptions' and 'notes'.

What to do
This activity works best when the children can see a vet in action, or talk to a visitor about the work of a vet. Encourage the children to think of questions to help them find out more, for example, 'Why do dogs need injections every year?', 'How does the stethoscope work?', 'Do animals have the same medicines as us?' and so on. Support your visitor by helping to find easy ways of making things understood.

Follow the visit up at story time with any stories and pictures you have about animals and vets. Ask questions such as, 'Why should we take care of animals?', 'What happens when they are not well?' and so on.

Now involve the children in helping you to set up a vet's surgery in your play area. Adapt your toy medical kit using toy syringes, stethoscopes and thermometers. Other props might include soft toys, animal baskets and bedding, a surgical table, feeding bottles and so on.

Special support
Use the activity to talk individually about caring.

Extension
Link the activity to a topic on pets or farming and ask the children for ideas on how to develop the vet's surgery to encompass their interests.

LEARNING
OBJECTIVE FOR ALL
THE CHILDREN
● to begin to ask
about and know
about the cultures
and rules of their
early years group.

**INDIVIDUAL
BEHAVIOUR TARGET**
● to think of and
abide by an
appropriate nursery
rule.

LINKS WITH HOME
If the approach seems
to be effective,
encourage parents
and carers to do a
similar activity at
home. Suggest that
they set a few very
clear rules, gain their
children's attention
and point to the sign
when they need to. If
this is paired with
strong verbal praise,
it can be an effective
way of changing
behaviour when
parents and carers
feel they have got
into a 'nagging cycle'.

Golden rules

Group size
Ten to twelve children.

What you need
Illustrations of familiar road signs; sheets of card (30cm x 30cm); coloured
pens; staple gun or drawing pins (adult use); the photocopiable sheet
on page 92.

What to do
Gather the children
together on the
floor. Ask them if
they know what a
'rule' is. Talk about
rules, using
contexts and
examples that they
may be able to
relate to, such as
road safety, people
stealing things or
people hurting
others. How do
rules help
everybody? Talk
about how rules
help people not to
harm one another
so that everybody can be safe and happy. Now talk about your group.
What rules are needed to help everybody feel happy? Try to arrive at
four to six very simple rules that the children have contributed to and
which seem right for your setting. Use the photocopiable sheet on page
92 to inspire ideas, such as: be happy; be friends; tidy up when you
finish; don't run indoors and so on.

Now show the children your road signs. Talk about how people can
be reminded to stick to the rules on the roads by looking at the signs.
Ask the children for ideas of what you might draw on your cards to
make signs linked to your nursery rules. Draw a sign for each of your
rules using the red surround and diagonal line typical of road signs.

Special support
Mount the signs onto the wall and point to the relevant sign when you
feel that a child is in danger of breaking a rule. Praise the child for
complying. This procedure can save a lot of 'nagging' and give the
children time to put their own actions right.

Extension
Introduce road signs into your outdoor vehicle play area. Help the
children to paint these themselves.

Rain drain

Group size
All the children, four to six at a time.

What you need
A wide selection of craft materials and containers – yoghurt pots, cans, bottles, boxes, funnels, dishes; permanent marker pen (adult use); measuring cylinder; tray.

What to do
Gather the children together on a rainy day and invite them to invent a machine to catch the rain. Suggest that they experiment today so that

they can find the best designs. What do they think they would use? Support each child as they decide what they are going to make and how to make it. At this stage, allow them to learn by trial and error; cardboard boxes are fine! Allow each child to make several machines if they wish to – this might all be part of their own 'experimenting'. Use name labels or descriptions so that the machines are easily identified. When all the machines are finished, place them out in the rain on a tray.

Later, bring the machines in and talk about which ones worked best. For example, perhaps the plastic cups have toppled over, or the cardboard boxes have become soggy and lost their water. Show the children how you can use a measuring cylinder to find out which 'machine' has caught the most rain. Talk about what they have learned and help them to plan again. Repeat the activity next time it rains and complete your 'experiment'.

Special support
It is important to support the child that you are targeting in this activity so that they feel safe in not 'getting it right' first time – they need to feel safe to learn from mistakes. Also support them in learning from the other children's mistakes so that they can design a brilliant machine second time around.

Extension
Set up a weather station to measure rainfall, wind speed and air temperature and encourage the children to find ways of recording their findings.

LEARNING OBJECTIVES FOR ALL THE CHILDREN
- to build and construct a device for collecting the rain
- to select the tools and techniques they need.

INDIVIDUAL BEHAVIOUR TARGETS
- to plan ahead
- to develop pride in their creations.

LINKS WITH HOME
Send the second designs home – these will have been perfected and so the children will feel justly proud of them!

LEARNING OBJECTIVE FOR ALL THE CHILDREN

● to observe, find out about and identify features in the place where they play and learn.

INDIVIDUAL BEHAVIOUR TARGET

● to be familiar with the physical boundaries of the setting and the rules for behaviour.

LINKS WITH HOME
Talk with parents and carers about boundaries at home. Where is it safe to go and where not? Look for some simple rules for carers to share with their children such as 'You can go out but you must stay in the square and you must come home when I call'.

Setting the boundaries

Group size
Three to four children.

What you need
A special guide's hat and big badge for yourself; toy microphone (if available); access to all your play areas inside and outside (so choose a dry day).

What to do
Gather the children together for a 'finding out' tour of the setting. Include the child that you are targeting. Explain that you will be the children's guide for the tour and put on your hat and badge. Make a flamboyant display of walking around the play area, commenting on the various children and their activities as you meet them, such as '…and here we have *Joe* pouring in the sand…'. Emphasize any rules you might have, again mentioning the children positively by name: '…and *Sula* knows that this sign here means that only three children can play at the water tray at once…'. If you see children breaking a rule, invite your targeted child to help you: 'Oh dear, ladies and gentlemen, here we see a problem. What do we say about sharing? My friend here will help me remember…'. Look for ways of reinforcing the rules as you move around.

Now go outside and walk the boundaries, using your 'tour' to explain exactly where the children may play. Explain, still in role, why the boundary needs to be kept safe.

Special support
This approach has the advantage of reinforcing rules and boundaries without having to confront a child already in the position of breaking them. Children who tend to break rules frequently can nevertheless learn to pay attention to them and be very effective 'policers' of their own environment with your support. Follow up by praising your targeted child by name for remembering the rules and boundaries.

Extension
Invite older children to help you as guides.

Treasure map

Group size
Six children.

What you need
An adult helper; story-book about pirates, such as *Captain Teachum's Buried Treasure* by Peter Carter and Paul Korky (Oxford University Press); box to resemble a treasure chest; 'treasure' (beads, bottle tops or 'coins', beakers covered in silver foil, and so on); paper; washable felt-tipped pens; toy parrot.

What to do
Use story time to introduce the topic of pirates to the children. Talk to them about how pirates buried their treasure.

When the children are playing outside, invite a few (including the child that you are targeting) to join you indoors to set up a game. Ensure that a helper remains with the rest of the group outside. Show the 'inside' group your 'treasure' and decide together where you will hide it. Support the children as each draws a 'map' showing how to find the treasure, starting with the outside door and showing the main features of the room. Ask them to make their maps as helpful as possible so that all the treasure can be rescued. You will have to help here by adding any details the child asks you to. Give your targeted child the parrot and suggest that they help the others to find the treasure by making the parrot squawk loudly whenever they go near any of the pieces. Invite groups of two or three children at a time to come indoors and follow one of the maps.

Special support
Give the child that you are targeting a key role in looking after the 'helpful parrot'.

Extension
Invite older children to each map their journey to the setting, or to draw a plan of their home and neighbourhood.

LINKS WITH HOME
Make sure that you tell parents and carers how helpful the parrot was! Ask them to add their own praise for their children who played and co-operated so well within the group.

Friends and neighbours

Group size
All the children, three or four at a time.

What you need
Coloured sugar paper; paints; paintbrushes; mounting paper; scissors and staple gun (adult use).

What to do
Introduce the activity when you are sitting all together during circle time. Who knows what a 'neighbour' is? Which children live near to each other? Do you have a friend who lives near to you? Do you know who your neighbours are? Who has children living next door to them? Explain that you will be making a large frieze showing where everyone lives and who their neighbours are.

In groups of three to four, invite each child to select paper and paints and to paint a picture of their home and their neighbours' homes. As they work, talk together about friends and neighbours. How do you know when someone is your friend? How do you become a 'good' neighbour?

When the paintings are dry, ask for the children's help as you mount them on the wall, adding your own landmarks to make a frieze of your community, village or area of town.

Special support
Take the opportunity to talk about friendly behaviour. Encourage the child that you are targeting to come up with their own ideas as to what makes a 'good' neighbour. Help them to discover that everyone has feelings and that we affect one another through our own behaviours. If they show signs of prejudice – for example, 'I swore at him because he's different from us' – turn the situation around and role-play what it must feel like from the other perspective. Model friendly behaviour and praise the child for behaving that way in the setting.

Extension
Build this activity into your map-making activity (see page 62) by inviting the children to draw maps of their neighbourhoods.

LEARNING OBJECTIVES FOR ALL THE CHILDREN
● to find out about the uses of everyday technology
● to use information and communication technology to support their learning.

INDIVIDUAL BEHAVIOUR TARGET
● to look carefully and to control impulsive behaviour.

Surfing

Group size
All the children, one child at a time.

What you need
A computer which is connected to the Internet; some of the interactive activities accessed on the Internet also require a plug-in.

What to do
Take one child at a time and switch the computer on. Show them which keys to press or how and where to click the mouse in order to get onto the Internet. If you are not sure yourself, make sure that a colleague

shows you how! You can start by typing in this address for the child, inviting them to press the 'return' key at the end:

www.bbc.co.uk/education

Show the child how to move the mouse and allow them to explore by clicking the mouse on the various symbols. If you need to, gently guide their hand.

Now guide the child towards a site which might be of interest to them. Look out for the icon of any familiar children's programme, such as *Tweenies*. You might find other icons there which will link you to 'Story Time', 'Messy Time' or 'Song Time'.

Special support
Make sure that the child remains calm and take care that they are actually thinking ahead and not clicking impulsively. If necessary, ask them to show you what to do, so that you can control the pace. Spend time playing the games together – the use of the computer will make them particularly motivating.

Extension
Explore other websites together. Use the Internet as a resource for pictures and facts. Try writing to an 'e-pen-friend'!

LINKS WITH HOME
Ask parents and carers to keep a note of any websites that their children have enjoyed. Keep a list of these near to your computer for easy reference.

PHYSICAL DEVELOPMENT

These activities will help all the children to develop confidence and skills in this area. Some of the ideas use children as special helpers and are therefore helpful in building self-esteem and confidence. Others teach careful and controlled movements.

LEARNING OBJECTIVE FOR ALL THE CHILDREN
● to move with confidence and safety.

INDIVIDUAL BEHAVIOUR TARGET
● to think carefully about their actions before moving.

Tumbling Ted

Group size
Eight to ten children.

What you need
All your usual PE equipment laid out in the hall, or your outdoor play equipment (climbing frame, slide, bikes and so on); large teddy bear.

What to do
Take the child that you are targeting into the hall or outdoor play area. Introduce the child to 'Tumbling Ted' and then teach Ted how to use each apparatus or play equipment safely. With your help, ask the child to demonstrate to Ted how to play safely, one piece of equipment at a time. Make Ted 'thank' the child profusely for each piece of advice or demonstration. Give Ted to the child to look after.

Now gather all the children and ask the child that you are targeting to introduce 'Tumbling Ted'. Move around the equipment as Tumbling Ted (helped by the child) demonstrates how to use each piece safely. Invite all the children to take turns to use the equipment, showing that they have understood the safety rules. Help your targeted child to make Ted clap his paws.

Special support
If the child makes Ted become 'silly', then tell Ted to play safely and ask the child to demonstrate again to Ted how to use the equipment correctly. Praise the child for doing it properly, giving more attention to the appropriate behaviour than the silliness and encouraging all the children to clap.

Extension
Ask the children to think of their own safety ideas for each piece of equipment. Draw up some simple rules together and write them down, representing them with pictures.

LINKS WITH HOME
Tell parents and carers that you have been talking about playing safely in your setting. Send home a simple ideas sheet about playing safely at home and ask carers to talk about it with their children.

LEARNING OBJECTIVES FOR ALL THE CHILDREN

● to move with control and co-ordination
● to show awareness of space, of themselves and of others.

INDIVIDUAL BEHAVIOUR TARGET

● to watch and mirror another child.

LINKS WITH HOME

Suggest that the parents or carers of any targeted children play a mirroring game with them. Can they copy closing a door *quietly*, or stroking the baby's hair *gently*, or walking *sensibly* along the pavement?

Disco doubles

Group size
Up to sixteen children.

What you need
Two adult helpers; open space; CD or tape player and some lively music (preferably from the current music charts); coloured bands; an even number of each colour (for example, four red, four green, four yellow, four blue).

What to do
Divide your bands into two identical sets. Give half the children a coloured band from the first set each. Within this half of your group, there should be the older children or those who find it easier to behave appropriately. Ask each child to go and find a space ready to do some disco dancing. Call this group 'The Cools' (or some such label!).

In your second group, include any children who need particular support, encouragement or help. Give each child in this group a coloured band and ask them to find their partner in the first group – the one with the same colour – and stand beside them. Call this group 'The Dudes' (or whatever you choose!).

Start the music and invite each child to dance with their partner until the music stops. Now ask the children to sit down and watch you. Ask one adult to dance as you stand in front and mirror everything they do. Invite 'The Cools' to copy 'The Dudes' as you start the music once more.

Finally, invite 'The Dudes' to copy 'The Cools'.

Special support
By dividing the children into groups in this way, you will be ensuring that children who need support are partnered to those who can provide helpful models. Stay close to your targeted child so that you can help them control any impulsive behaviour, and praise any co-operative behaviour. If a child begins to disrupt, ask them to sit at the side for one piece of the music and then try again, stating the rules clearly.

Extension
Play some ballet music and encourage the children to move and mirror their partners as they move slowly and expressively.

LEARNING OBJECTIVE FOR ALL THE CHILDREN
● to move with confidence, imagination and in safety.

INDIVIDUAL BEHAVIOUR TARGET
● to look ahead before they leap!

LINKS WITH HOME
Suggest a game for keeping lively children 'focused' on the way home – not to tread on the lines of the paving stones!

Jumping Jacks

Group size
Six children.

What you need
A wide open space; about ten hoops (at least one metre in diameter); a beanbag for each child.

What to do
Arrange the hoops in a circle on the floor, each hoop should be one child's large stride apart from the next. Ask the children to watch as you throw your beanbag into the next hoop and, once it has landed, jump into that hoop without touching the rest of the floor. Explain that you can only throw your beanbag into a hoop if there is no one in it. Now ask a child to have a turn, slowly moving around the circle as they throw their beanbag and then jump. Start the next child after the first has reached the third or fourth hoop and pace the rest of the children in the same way.

Now invite the children to arrange all the hoops differently in the space provided as they work out several different routes for travelling from one side of the room to another. Can the children throw their beanbags a little bit further this time?

Special support
Stay close to any child that you are targeting. Praise them for throwing and jumping carefully and for not moving into any hoop where there is a child already. If any of the children become disruptive during the game, gently lead them to one side to watch and then invite them to try again later.

Extension
Let the children all move around the hoop circle together, working out themselves how to occupy the spaces safely.

LEARNING OBJECTIVE FOR ALL THE CHILDREN
● to use a range of small equipment.

INDIVIDUAL BEHAVIOUR TARGET
● to plan ahead and aim with care.

Speckled frogs

Group size
Five children.

What you need
The photocopiable sheet on page 93; A4 sheet of card; glue; tailor's chalk; five green beanbags; green felt; twelve buttons for eyes; hoop; transparent plastic film; scissors; needle and thread (adult use).

What to do
Photocopy the photocopiable sheet on page 93 and glue it onto an A4 sheet of card. Cut out the frog's arms and legs (you will need to reverse them for the second pair so that you have two right limbs and two left) to make templates.

Gather the children around a table and explain that you are going to make some 'beanie' frogs which will live in the nursery. Show them the frog at the top of the photocopiable sheet so that they can see what they are going to make. Help them to use the tailor's chalk to draw around the templates onto green felt. Cut out the limbs for the children. Show them the green beanbags, or frogs' bodies, and encourage each child in turn to show you where to attach the legs and arms as you add some stitches to hold them in place. Sew on two eyes to complete them.

Now have fun together as you wrap the plastic film around the hoop, making a 'pool' of water for your handmade frogs.

Gather the children around as you sing 'Five Little Frogs', from *Apusskidu* chosen by Beatrice Harrop (A & C Black). Hold the hoop steady, asking the child that you are targeting to throw their frog into the pool during the first verse. Now invite that child to help you hold the hoop, using two hands. Sing the verses and invite a new child to throw another frog into the pond for each verse.

Special support
By inviting the child that you are targeting to help, you will be giving them a clear task to do, focusing their hands and attention, and boosting their self-esteem.

Extension
Make crêpe-paper lilies and plants for your 'habitat'.

LINKS WITH HOME
Send a beanbag frog and a hoop home for the child to play an aiming game with their parents or carers, throwing the frog into the 'pool' as they gradually move further away from it.

Superheroes

Group size
Four children.

What you need
Equipment to make an obstacle course (a tunnel, cardboard boxes to climb through, hoops to step between, a duvet to dive beneath, a bench to wiggle along, soft play blocks to weave between and so on); mats for safety; large 'superhero' stickers or rosettes; additional adult helpers; (toy) commentator's megaphone.

What to do
If you do not have suitable stickers or rosettes, make these with the children at an earlier session. Arrange the equipment into an obstacle course, bearing in mind the capabilities and behaviour of the children so that you can plan it safely. Consider where you might need additional adult helpers or safety mats.

First, take your targeted child around the course, giving your individual attention. Show how each piece of equipment can be manoeuvred. Ask them if they would like to demonstrate the course to the other children.

Gather the children together and tell them that you are going to set them a 'superhero challenge'. Invite your 'helper' to demonstrate the course, praising them for being sensible but taking over if they become disruptive. Invite the children to set off, one at a time, as you provide an enthusiastic commentary, using the megaphone: 'Now Sayeed is *over* the bench; he's *under* the cover; he's *through* the tunnel...' and so on. Pretend to be timing each child and encourage all the children to cheer at the finish. Invite other children to take a turn with the megaphone, emphasizing the position words. Enjoy a presentation of stickers or rosettes at the end.

Special support
This activity gives your targeted child every chance of succeeding in front of their peers. If they have been really helpful, suggest that they present the stickers to their friends at the end.

Extension
Encourage older children to design and set up the course. Talk about safety together.

LEARNING OBJECTIVES FOR ALL THE CHILDREN
● to use a range of large equipment
● to travel around, under, over and through balancing and climbing equipment.

INDIVIDUAL BEHAVIOUR TARGETS
● to move carefully and safely
● to develop positive self-esteem.

LINKS WITH HOME
Make sure that the parents or carers know why their child has a sticker and encourage them to show how proud they are. Present your targeted child with a special sticker for being your helper and explain to their parents how helpful they have been.

LEARNING OBJECTIVE FOR ALL THE CHILDREN
● to recognize the changes that happen to their bodies when active and when still.

INDIVIDUAL BEHAVIOUR TARGET
● to stay still when appropriate.

LINKS WITH HOME
Tell the parents or carers how still their child sat. Suggest that they challenge their child to sit still for five whole minutes at tea-time and tell you the next day if they managed it.

Sitting still

Group size
Four to six children.

What you need
A tambourine; stethoscope (or disposable plastic cup); wide open space for moving in.

What to do
Gather the children together and talk about their bodies. What happens when they move their bodies a lot? What do they notice when they run? Suggest that you find out together. Tell the children that when they hear the tambourine, they should run very quickly on the spot. Show them what 'on the spot' means. When you beat it loudly, they should stop.

Shake your tambourine as you all pound your feet quickly. Just when you are beginning to puff and pant a bit, give a sharp bang and suggest that you all sit down. What is happening to your bodies? Prompt the children if necessary by asking them to think about their breathing. Can anyone feel their heart beating? Spend a few minutes listening to one another's heartbeats with the stethoscope (or by putting your ear to a plastic cup held over someone's heart). Can they hear how quickly the hearts are beating? Now suggest that you see what happens when you sit still. As the children sit quietly, talk together about their breathing and listen to their heartbeats again.

Special support
Stay close to any child that you are targeting and praise them for staying still. Listen to their heartbeat and tell them how still they must be keeping.

Be aware of any child with exercise-induced asthma and make sure that they pace themselves.

Extension
Explain, in simple terms, how the body needs air and food to move. The heart pumps the blood full of air all around the body so it reaches the parts that move. When you sit still, the heart does not have to work so fast and you do not need to breathe in so much air.

LEARNING OBJECTIVE FOR ALL THE CHILDREN
● to use a range of small equipment.

INDIVIDUAL BEHAVIOUR TARGET
● to develop confidence in front of a group of other children.

LINKS WITH HOME
Invite parents and carers to arrive ten minutes early to enjoy the spectacle. Encourage them to laugh and applaud with the entertainers and tell their children how well they performed.

Circus capers

Group size
All the children, but three or four at a time.

What you need
Hoops; dowelling rods (one metre long); paper plates; glue; small sponge balls; elastic; upholstery needle (adult use); dressing-up clothes; large shoes; face paints; general craft and collage materials for additional decorations and embellishments.

What to do
Start by talking about clowns and circuses with the children. Have any of them seen a clown, in real life, or on television? Show the group a picture book or an illustration if possible. Why do clowns make us laugh? Suggest that you all practise some clown tricks to make the parents and carers laugh at home-time.

Invite small groups of children to explore your dressing-up box for anything suitable. Try on big shoes and clothes and make yourselves look as funny as possible by painting your faces with the face paints.

Now decide on your tricks. Help each child to choose what they would like to do. For example, they could:
● be jugglers (use your upholstery needle to thread elastic through four sponge balls, knotting between each one; when jiggled, they will look as if they are being juggled);
● spin plates (glue a paper plate to the end of a piece of dowelling; decorate it for extra effect);
● spin a hula hoop (use elastic to tie the hoop to the child's shoulders so that when they twist it turns about a little bit);
● walk on their hands (with an adult holding around their waist, 'wheelbarrow' style).
Practise your tricks and get ready for a grand performance!

Special support
Children who love attention can earn it by joining in very appropriately. Be aware of any child who is frightened of costumes and props, providing extra reassurance if necessary.

Extension
Invite the children to come up with their own ideas for tricks.

LEARNING OBJECTIVE FOR ALL THE CHILDREN
● to move with safety.

INDIVIDUAL BEHAVIOUR TARGET
● to move without bumping into other children and obstacles.

Treading carefully

Group size
Eight to ten children.

What you need
Some crinkly paper which makes a noise if you tread on it; clothes (or artwork) drying rack; selection of jingle bells and shakers; string.

What to do
Ask the child that you are targeting to help you by crumpling up paper and holding shakers as you attach string to them. Tie some string across the room and suspend a selection of rattles, shakers and bells from it so that the children have to bend down to avoid them. Place the paper around the floor so that it can be stepped around, and arrange the drying rack in the way with more noise-making instruments attached to it. Your challenge is now set up.

Invite your helper to try to move across the room without moving any of the shakers or bells and without stepping on the paper. Provide

plenty of support and encouragement, reminding them of the need to tread carefully.

Gather the children around and invite your helper to show them how to manoeuvre the obstacles without making a sound. All sit very quietly as each child moves through. Tell the children that you are closing your eyes and listening for any sound, but make sure that there is another pair of adult eyes watching all the time!

Special support
This is an activity where you can engage the child as a helper, encouraging their co-operation and boosting their self-esteem. It is also a good way of teaching careful, thoughtful movement to all the children.

Extension
Pass bells and shakers around a circle, challenging the children not to make a sound.

LINKS WITH HOME
Show parents and carers how they can play 'Grandmother's footsteps' – the adult shuts their eyes, the child should move silently towards the adult, and the adult may only open their eyes to catch the child if they hear a sound.

Lying low

Group size
Eight to ten children.

What you need
A large open space; the rhyme below.

What to do
Gather the children together with plenty of space around them and teach them the rhyme below:

> Down in the swamps where we don't go
> Hundreds of crocodiles lying low
> Some looking cross and some looking happy
> Some looking hungry and some looking…
> …SNAPPY!
>
> *Hannah Mortimer*

Now ask the children to lie down quietly on their tummies with their arms stretched out to the front, with their palms together. Show them how to snap their hands together to imitate the snapping of the crocodile's jaws. Now tell the 'crocodiles' that it is time to lie low as they wait very, very quietly for their dinner. Explain that if they make a noise, their dinner will run away!

Chant the rhyme very quietly and slowly. Spend a moment or two walking among the crocodiles to see just how quiet and still they are. Pause after the word 'looking…' and encourage all the crocodiles to snap for the last word.

Chant the rhyme again, encouraging the children to lie very, very quietly until the end. Praise them for keeping so still.

Special support
If necessary, suggest that a key worker lies beside a child who is going to find it hard to settle and help them to cope with the suspense without the child becoming too excited.

Extension
Encourage the childrent o help you find out about crocodiles, where they live and what they usually eat.

LEARNING OBJECTIVE FOR ALL THE CHILDREN
● to move with control and imagination.

INDIVIDUAL BEHAVIOUR TARGET
● to move slowly and quietly when appropriate.

LINKS WITH HOME
If this rhyme was popular with the children, suggest that parents and carers distract them by playing the 'Crocodile' game at home when the situation is getting too noisy.

LEARNING OBJECTIVE FOR ALL THE CHILDREN
● to recognize the importance of keeping healthy and those foods which contribute to this.

INDIVIDUAL BEHAVIOUR TARGETS
● to develop a liking for healthy and natural foods
● to inform parents and carers about healthy diets.

LINKS WITH HOME
Ask parents and carers to help you with suggestions and make sure that you sample a wide range of foods from different cultures and countries of origin.

What goes in...

Group size
All the children.

What you need
Old food magazines; scissors; glue; selection of healthy foods to eat (such as fruit, vegetables, breads and natural foods); A3 sheet of paper.

What to do
For the first session, work with groups of four or five at a table. Talk about foods which are good for you and foods which are not so good for you. What are the children's favourite foods? Are these foods healthy or not so healthy? Which foods do the children dislike? Why do they dislike them?

Look through the magazines and help the children to cut out pictures of healthy foods and not so healthy foods. Build up a collage by sticking pictures of healthy foods on one side of the sheet of paper, and pictures of not so healthy food on the other.

For the second session, bring in a selection of healthy foods for the children to sample. Wash and cut up suitable fruit and raw vegetables. Sample different breads and staple foods. Try salads and natural fruit juices. Plan together your favourite snacks and use these to replace any 'biscuit time' you normally have. (NB Check for any dietary requirements and food allergies – see 'Special support'.)

Special support
Be aware that some children with behavioural and emotional difficulties react to certain foods. Make sure that you ask all parents and carers if their children are allergic or reactive to anything. It is usually the natural, unprocessed (and therefore more healthy) foods which are best for calm behaviour.

Extension
Help the children to make up their own salad plates to take home, made up of their favourite healthy snacks.

CREATIVE DEVELOPMENT

These activities will help all the children to develop creatively. Explore colours, shapes, sounds, touch and smell using a range of art, craft, music and movement. There are suggestions for encouraging appropriate behaviour and co-operation.

LEARNING OBJECTIVE FOR ALL THE CHILDREN
● to use their imagination in designing a movement game.

INDIVIDUAL BEHAVIOUR TARGETS
● to work co-operatively in a small group
● to develop positive self-esteem.

Boot prints

Group size
All the children, four at a time.

What you need
A hard playground outside which can be painted on; outdoor masonry paint and paint tray; large pair of old wellington boots; wellington boots for the children; basin of water; chalk.

What to do
Wait for a sunny day. Share the joke of putting on your wellington boots in the fine weather and take the group outside.

Show the children how they can wet their boots in the basin and then make wet prints on the ground. Suggest that they make tracks and follow one another. What does it look like when they jump or hop? Look

at the boot prints together and talk about how they evaporate in the sun. Now put your big boots on and see if you can reproduce some of the patterns that the children have made – a walk, some jumps, some hops. Can the children follow in your boot steps, copying the same movements by stepping on your prints?

Ask the children how they might make the boot prints stay – painting them would be one way. Design a 'boot-print track' together, marking it with your wet boots and asking the children to draw a big circle around each wet outline with chalk.

Go back outside when all is quiet and the children have gone home, and paint the boot prints with the masonry paints, making them a permanent reminder of your activity in the playground.

Special support
Invite a key worker to hold the child's hand if necessary. Accept any good ideas and value them. Focus the child onto the permanent boot prints when you go out to play to distract them from any play which is becoming too active or aggressive.

Extension
Let the children make paint boot prints on long strips of paper indoors.

LINKS WITH HOME
Suggest a basin of water and a brush for 'water painting' on paving stones at home when the weather is sunny.

LEARNING OBJECTIVES FOR ALL THE CHILDREN
● to use their imagination in music
● to recognize and explore how sounds can be changed.

INDIVIDUAL BEHAVIOUR TARGETS
● to look and listen within a group
● to develop positive self-esteem in front of their peers.

LINKS WITH HOME
Include cassettes and CDs in your book library for the children to borrow and take home, perhaps booking out an instrument to borrow too. Teach parents and carers the 'Start and stop' game.

Lead the band

Group size
Ten to twelve children.

What you need
A selection of percussion instruments: bells, shakers, drums, scrapers, tambourines, blocks and so on; cassette or CD player with an assortment of music.

What to do
Use this activity at the end of circle time or song time. Save the musical instruments until the end of your session, placing them in a box to one side of the circle. Tell the children when it is time for the instruments. Explain that you are looking for children who are sitting up straight and waiting quietly. Pick out children by name: 'Nazia, you are sitting beautifully, come and choose an instrument'; 'Lee, you are waiting quietly, come and choose one too'. When each child has an instrument, explain that you would like them to play when you play and stop when you stop. Start the cassette or CD player and play your own instrument too. After 20 seconds or so, stop the music and look around at all the children. Praise them for listening and for stopping, and have a few turns until they are really good at this.

Continue by suggesting that the children take turns at starting and stopping the band, either by playing their instruments or making a 'halt' sign with their hands to stop everyone. Let a few children, including the child that you are targeting, take a turn at being the leader.

Special support
Sometimes, there might be one child who starts when the others stop, watching for the reaction they will get. Suggest that you are going to start when that child starts and stop when he or she stops. You will have thus 'brought into line' the contrary child and you are all joining in appropriately again.

Extension
Choose one of the children to be the 'conductor' and let them bring in or stop whole sections of bells or tambourines by pointing to them or giving a 'halt' sign.

LEARNING OBJECTIVES FOR ALL THE CHILDREN
● to explore how sounds can be changed
● to use their imagination when creating sounds.

INDIVIDUAL BEHAVIOUR TARGET
● to release emotions appropriately.

LINKS WITH HOME
If a child is terrified of thunder storms, suggest that the parents or carers keep a 'thunder bowl' (an aluminium bowl and spoon) in a convenient cupboard. When there is thunder, they can encourage their child to make more noise than the thunder outside. This gives the child a 'job to do' when they are afraid and can therefore help them to overcome their fear.

I hear thunder

Group size
Ten to twenty children.

What you need
Aluminium bowls or pans; wooden spoons; sound-making objects such as a thunder board (a sheet of metal which, when flexed, makes a rumble of thunder), or washboard and wooden spoon; big drums, rainmakers.

What to do
Place the instruments and sound-making objects to one side in a box. Start by teaching the children the song below to the tune of 'Frère Jacques':

> I hear thunder, I hear thunder,
> Hark, don't you? Hark, don't you?
> Pitter-patter raindrops, pitter-patter raindrops,
> I'm wet through, SO ARE YOU!
>
> *Traditional*

Spend some time talking about thunderstorms. Has anyone seen or heard one? Was it exciting? Was it scary? What did it sound like? What did it look like?

Introduce the box of instruments and suggest that the children experiment with different sounds and find some which could be used to go with the song. Ask individuals to demonstrate their sounds to you. Help the children to organize themselves as far as they can, and when they are ready, sing the rhyme again, pausing between each line to make the sound effects.

Special support
Encourage a very timid child to choose a very loud drum, and a very energetic child to experiment with soft sounds as well as loud.

Extension
Make up a sound story about a walk through a storm. Encourage the children to select appropriate instruments and make the sounds to accompany your words.

LEARNING OBJECTIVE FOR ALL THE CHILDREN
- to respond in a variety of ways to what they see, hear, touch and feel.

INDIVIDUAL BEHAVIOUR TARGET
- to feel calmed and to regain control over their reactions.

LINKS WITH HOME
If this approach is effective for any child with behavioural and emotional difficulties, look for ways of lifting the ideas into the home situation. Use the photocopiable sheet on page 94.

The special place

Group size
One child (as they need it).

What you need
A special corner in your nursery with soft cushions, fabrics, a drape to make a 'cave' across the corner (so that you can still be seen inside); calming music, such as *Tubular Bells* by Mike Oldfield (Dabringhaus und Grimm); beautiful

things to look at and feel; a special cuddly toy; adult 'on duty' to provide comfort as needed (and to 'talk' via the toy).

What to do
Spend time as a group collecting beautiful things for your special corner. Tell the children that it should be a place to go to whenever they are feeling upset or sad. Can they think of things to look at, listen to, or touch that might help them feel better? Encourage all the children to respect this corner and to keep it beautiful and calm. Explain that if an adult and a child are in the special place, then we should keep away and give them time to feel better.

Whenever a child is troubled, suggest that you spend time in the special place together. Invite the children to go there themselves if they need to be quiet. The adult 'on duty' should always approach a child there and ask if they would like company. This should be repeated regularly, talking gently with them or reading a distracting story if they are still there after ten minutes or so.

Special support
As a key worker gets to know a targeted child, they should become aware of the times when the child needs space to stay calm or to deal with their emotions. The special place can be used to prevent situations from escalating into full-blown tantrums by withdrawing to it before the escalation.

If a child has already had a full-blown tantrum, withdraw with them to a separate room until they have calmed down, avoiding eye contact and direct attention, and then move into the special place as a way of restoring calm and rewarding the end of the tantrum.

Extension
Encourage older children to think of ideas for your special place.

Sticky fingers

Group size
Three or four children.

What you need
Water-based glue in a pot; dishes with glitter; tiny metallic stars and shiny shapes; pieces of coloured feathers; tiny shreds of coloured tissue paper; basin of warm soapy water; towels; camera.

What to do
Invite the children to sit around a table. Show them how you can decorate a finger by dipping it into the glue and then into a dish of glitter or shiny shapes. Explain that this involves very careful finger movements. Decorate two of your fingers in different ways, then invite each child to decorate one of their own fingers, encouraging gentle movements and control when dipping into the dishes and pots. Help the children to develop their own ideas – some might like to make faces and others brilliant patterns.

Take photographs of the finished products before the children wash their hands at the end.

Special support
Some children become quickly distressed when they feel their fingers becoming sticky. These children need plenty of experience in feeling and touching. They need to be encouraged to stay relaxed and playful as they do so, in order to become less sensitive to touch. They also need to know that 'it is OK' to get dirty sometimes. If a child is very anxious, have a quick dab and then wash their hands, praising them for joining in. Return to the activity another time to take it one step further.

Extension
Use the tips of rubber gloves and substitute latex glue for a more permanent product. You can make a selection of finger puppets or 'fireworks' in this way for a puppet play or as props for a story or rhyme.

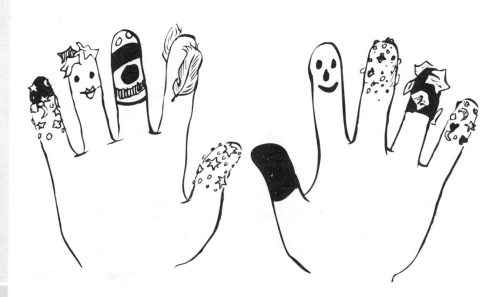

LINKS WITH HOME
If you need to, explain that some children are still at an early stage of wanting to touch and feel things, and that this is why they might be messy eaters at mealtimes. Help parents and carers to sort out which behaviours are 'naughty' and which are simply because their children still like to fiddle and touch.

LEARNING OBJECTIVE FOR ALL THE CHILDREN
● to explore colour, texture and shape in three dimensions.

INDIVIDUAL BEHAVIOUR TARGETS
● to release emotional feelings appropriately
● to feel proud of their creations.

LINKS WITH HOME
Ask parents and carers to help prepare the eggshells.

Egg splats

Group size
Three or four children.

What you need
Clean eggshells, approximately in halves (left over from neatly cracked soft-boiled eggs); brightly coloured poster paints thickened with paste, in pots with teaspoons; solid chair for the children to stand on with an adult helper to support them; low table; large sheets of paper and newspaper; plenty of aprons and overalls; washing bowls; warm soapy water; towels.

What to do
Arrange newspapers all over the floor of your 'messy play' area. Remove other furniture and equipment to the side. Alternatively, save this activity for a sunny day and spread the newspapers over part of the playground. Place a low chair on the newspapers and a large sheet of paper behind it.

Place the eggshells, paint pots and spoons on a low table. Show the children how to handle the eggshells very gently without crushing them. Demonstrate to them how to spoon large drops of thick paint into each one. Support each child as they gently carry their shell of paint to the chair. Hold the chair while your helper supports the child standing up on it. Show the children how they can drop their shells onto the paper making a 'splat' picture. Lift the pictures carefully and place them somewhere flat to dry. Wash hands and wipe chairs!

Special support
This is a wonderful activity for releasing pent-up emotions. It is also helpful for teaching 'gentle' finger movements. Any targeted child will need a key worker with them all the time.

Extension
Add feathers and sparkly pieces for a more creative effect.

CREATIVE DEVELOPMENT • CREATIVE DEVELOPMENT

LEARNING OBJECTIVES FOR ALL THE CHILDREN
● to respond in a variety of ways to what they see, smell and feel
● to use their imagination in role-play.

INDIVIDUAL BEHAVIOUR TARGET
● to handle delicate objects gently.

LINKS WITH HOME
Make up tiny matchbox-sized treasure chests to take home. Ask parents and carers to encourage their children to tell them the 'story in the box'. Can the children make up treasure chests at home to bring in and share with the rest of the group?

Treasure chest

Group size
Four to six children.

What you need
A large box which looks like a pirate's treasure chest; collection of props inside the box, depending on the theme of your role-play.

What to do
Plan what you are going to have in the treasure chest before each session. One day you might have some pirates' hats, some 'jewels', an old map, a message in a bottle, a spyglass, a coconut and a piece of lace. Another day you might have a bucket and spade, sun-hats, a pair of sun-glasses, sun cream, a towel and a travel book. The idea is that the children will talk together, with your guidance, and find a link for all the items which will provide the theme of your role-play.

Gather the children around you and open the treasure chest together. Encourage them to lift out each item, and talk together about what it might be. Ask questions such as, 'Who do you think this chest belonged to?', 'What were they doing?', 'What happened to them?' and so on. Encourage the children to make up a story linking all the items. They will need plenty of guidance to help keep the story flowing! Help them to enjoy playing out the story and developing it imaginatively together.

Special support
Avoid toy weapons or items which might trigger aggressive play. Select interesting items for your chest which are going to attract the interest of all the children and make them ponder a little.

Extension
Encourage older children to help you put together the treasure chest, based on their own ideas and with your help and suggestions.

LEARNING OBJECTIVE FOR ALL THE CHILDREN
● to express and communicate their feelings by using a range of materials.

INDIVIDUAL BEHAVIOUR TARGET
● to release angry feelings appropriately.

LINKS WITH HOME
Suggest ways in which parents and carers can encourage angry children to become calmer, such as: big breaths; a count to five; punching a pillow; shouting the 'cross-ness' up a tree; a violent scribble and so on.

Letting it out

Group size
Two or three children.

What you need
Two huge sheets of paper mounted low on a wall, one red or orange and one blue or green; table; paints; glue; brushes; range of interesting collage materials.

What to do
Talk to the children about feelings and encourage them to share their thoughts. When do they feel angry? When do they feel quiet? Introduce the words 'calm' and 'peaceful'. Suggest that you make pictures together, one 'angry' picture and one 'calm' picture. Discuss what colours might be useful for each. How will the children make their pictures 'angry' or 'calm'?

Stay close to the children to support and encourage them as they try different colours, shapes and ways of painting to express themselves. Ask them to tell you all about what they are doing. Look for sharp, jagged shapes and edges to represent the anger, and for smooth, wavy lines and shapes to represent calm. Examine the effects of different colours and shapes as you try them out.

Special support
Suggest that the key worker plays alongside any targeted child, asking the child what they should do. The child might delegate tasks for the key worker to do, and as they work together, it becomes easier to talk about angry feelings and calm feelings.

Encourage the children to think about what they can do to make themselves calm when they feel angry.

Help the children to practise counting to five or taking big breaths to make themselves calm.

Extension
Suggest that older children make individual collages and paintings for a range of feelings.

Jungle howls

Group size
Ten to twenty children.

What to do
Familiarize yourself with this rhyme:

> Monsters in the jungle,
> Circling around;
> Growling at their friends and
> Clawing at the ground;
> Slowly, very slowly,
> In they creep
> Lifting up their heads to HOWLLLLLL!
>
> *Hannah Mortimer*

Gather the children in a circle, holding hands. Teach them the rhyme as you all circle slowly around, baring your teeth and pawing the ground for the fourth line.

Now slow the rhyme right down for the fifth line, creep slowly into the centre of the circle, still holding hands and crouching low. Raise your voices gradually through the last line as you raise your arms together. Hold your hands high for the last line as you howl to the sky. Return to your silent stalking at the end and repeat the rhyme!

Special support
Start with a small group of children first, so that any targeted child can see what is going to happen.

Allow any child who is frightened of noise to watch or stand back, or make up a quieter hissing version of the rhyme instead.

Invite the key worker of any child that you are targeting to take a position opposite the child in the circle, so that they can hold eye contact and encourage them for the final coming together and howling. Stand next to the child yourself so that you can hold their hand.

Extension
Ask the children to help you make up new verses with real jungle animals and sounds.

LEARNING OBJECTIVE FOR ALL THE CHILDREN
● to express and communicate their thoughts and feelings using imaginative role-play.

INDIVIDUAL BEHAVIOUR TARGETS
● to develop confidence in a group of children
● to develop confidence in using eye contact.

LINKS WITH HOME
Encourage the parents or carers of any targeted child to establish regular eye contact and to use their child's name before asking them to do something. If their child does not comply, suggest a '1, 2, 3...' warning, followed by gently leading the child through the action if they still do not obey. If the child complies, they should praise them warmly.

LEARNING OBJECTIVE FOR ALL THE CHILDREN
● to use their imagination in dance.

INDIVIDUAL BEHAVIOUR TARGET
● to develop positive self-esteem.

LINKS WITH HOME
Lend the magic wand to parents and carers. Suggest that they call 'bed-time, story time' and wave the wand to bring calm to a lively child ready to enjoy a cuddle and a story before sleep. It sometimes works!

Magic moments

Group size
Ten to twelve children.

What you need
A magician's cloak, hat and magic wand; CD player; music such as *The Sorcerer's Apprentice* by Dukas.

What to do
Take the children into an open space and tell them that you are going to play some music to them. Each time the music stops, you are going to pretend to make a magic spell and make them dance a different way.

Put on the cloak and hat. Wave your wand and tell them that you want them all to dance like… 'mice'! Play 20 seconds or so of music and then stop it. This time, 'turn' the children into 'elephants'!

Now invite the child that you are targeting to take a turn as your helper. Give them the cloak and hat. Whisper together to plan what you are going to turn the children into next, so that you can agree it is appropriate. Support the child as the wand is waved and help them to say the words 'I want you all to dance like…'.

Repeat six or seven times at the most. Finish by enjoying some free expression to the music.

Special support
This activity provides an audience for the child's appropriate behaviour, and boosts self-esteem and co-operation in the group.

Demonstrate the movements of the different animals for children who are a little unsure. Encourage them to copy you to give them the confidence to join in.

Extension
Encourage older children to take turns at being the magician, thinking up their own ideas. Vary it by trying emotions, for example, dance happily, dance crossly or dance tiredly.

Individual education plan

Name:	Early Years Action/Action Plus:

Nature of learning difficulty:

Action	Who will do what?
1. Seeking further information	
2. Seeking training or support	
3. Observations and assessments	
4. Managing the behaviour	

What exactly is the inappropriate behaviour we wish to change?

What behaviour do we wish to encourage instead?

What will we do in general to make appropriate behaviour more likely to occur?

What will we do whenever the inappropriate behaviour happens?

What will we do whenever the appropriate behaviour happens instead?

Help from parents or carers:

Targets for this term:

How will we measure whether we have achieved these?

Review meeting with parents or carers:

Who else to invite:

From Developing Individual Behaviour Plans in Early Years Settings by Hannah Mortimer (NASEN).

Planning sheet

1. What is the existing inappropriate behaviour you wish to change (in 'clear' words)?

2. What appropriate behaviour do you wish to see instead after the change?

3. How will you measure your 'baseline' and carry out your 'ABC analysis'?

4. Now you have done this, what **antecedents** tend to lead up to the inappropriate behaviour?

5. What are the **consequences** of this behaviour?

6. What rewarding events seem to work for the child?

7. Now write a clear individual behaviour plan showing how you will change the antecedents and the consequences of the behaviour in order to change the behaviour.

From *Developing Individual Behaviour Plans in Early Years Settings* by Hannah Mortimer (NASEN).

SPECIAL NEEDS **in the early years:** Behavioural and emotional difficulties

Not such a good morning

Eysha Elephant was having a lovely morning at playschool. First, she had painted a picture. Then she had read a story. Now she was playing with the train.

It was the nicest train Eysha had ever seen. It was red with blue wheels. It had a yellow wagon, which it pulled along. Eysha nudged the train gently along the track with her trunk. In her mind Eysha was telling the story of what was happening.

The train was on its way to the seaside. It had lots of animals on board. Sam Squirrel was there. And Pete Penguin. And Lotte Lion. They were all going to the seaside together, for a holiday. Eysha was pretending to be the engine driver, singing a happy song inside her head. 'La, li, la, li, la', she sang. 'Off we go to the seaside...'.

She was so busy, singing her song, being the engine driver and watching after the animals on board, that she didn't hear Eli Elephant coming up behind her.

'La, li, la, li, la', she sang.

And then, before she could even begin to think what was happening, Eli pushed rudely past her, elbowing her out of the way. And before Eysha could even utter a sound, Eli jumped up in the air on his four huge feet and crashed right down onto the train track.

The track broke up, bits of it going hither and thither all over the floor. The red engine with its blue wooden wheels somersaulted into the air and crashed back down again. And the little yellow wagon – the little yellow wagon with all the poor, poor animals in – smashed into a hundred pieces.

'Oh no!', Eysha looked up in amazement...

Irene Yates

Big voice, little voice

Say the words together using a little voice and then a big voice.

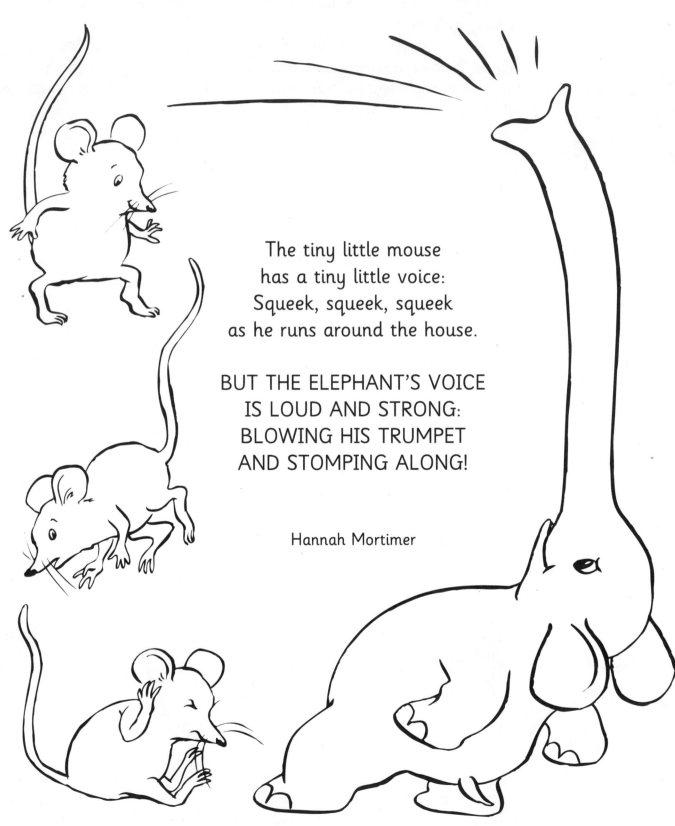

The tiny little mouse
has a tiny little voice:
Squeek, squeek, squeek
as he runs around the house.

BUT THE ELEPHANT'S VOICE
IS LOUD AND STRONG:
BLOWING HIS TRUMPET
AND STOMPING ALONG!

Hannah Mortimer

Dotty dominoes

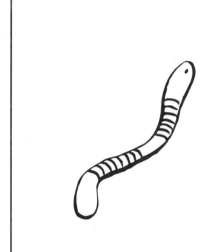

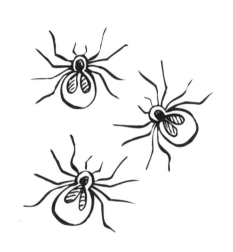

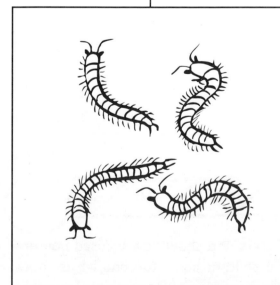

Celebration certificate

I have been BRILLIANT today because...

_____

_____

_____

_____

Here is my smiley face!

Parents or carers: Please talk to your child about this success and show how pleased you are with the good behaviour. Look for chances to praise your child at home too and let us know how you get on.

My story

Message for parents or carers

Dear _____

Next week we will be helping the children make little books about their lives. We find that this helps them to talk about the past and the present and to feel 'special'. We would be really grateful for your help.

   Could we borrow any photographs of the family and of your child when younger? We will use peelable glue so that you can reuse them and we promise to take care of them. Please write on the back your child's name and what the photograph shows.

   If you could tell us who is in the family, this will help us to ask the right questions. If there is anything we should not ask about, or anything you would like us to understand before we do this activity, please tell us.

My home and family

My mum's name: Photograph? YES/NO

My dad's name: Photograph? YES/NO

Other family members?   Photographs? YES/NO

My home   Photograph? YES/NO

Other homes I spend time in?   Photograph? YES/NO

Me as a baby   Photograph? YES/NO

Special times we have had?   Photograph? YES/NO

Anything else you would like in your book?   Photograph? YES/NO

Thank you so much for helping.

From:

Golden rules

Photocopy and enlarge these signs for reminders of your golden rules.

Be happy
Be friends
Tidy up when you finish
Look after the books
Don't run indoors
Don't throw things

SPECIAL NEEDS **in the early years:** Behavioural and emotional difficulties

Speckled frogs

Special things

Today, _____ felt very angry and yet managed to

calm down beautifully. We are very proud of _____ .

_____ went to our special place to be quiet and to

feel better.

These were the favourite things that helped to calm things down.

Favourite smell:

Favourite music:

Favourite book:

Favourite comforter:

When everything was calm and settled, we were able to talk about

what had gone wrong.

You might like to try these ideas at home.

RECOMMENDED RESOURCES

ORGANIZATIONS AND SUPPORT GROUPS

● ADHD Family Support Group, 1A High Street, Dilton Marsh, Westbury, Wiltshire BA14 4DL. Tel: 01373-826045.

● National NEWPIN, Sutherland House, 35 Sutherland Square, Walworth, London SE17 3EE. Tel: 020-77036326. NEWPIN is a national voluntary organization that helps parents under stress to break the cycle of destructive family behaviour.

● Association of Workers for Children with Emotional and Behavioural Difficulties (AWCEBD), Charlton Court, East Sutton, Maidstone, Kent ME17 3DQ. Tel: 01622-843104.

● The *CaF Directory* of specific conditions and rare syndromes in children (including those that affect behaviour) with their family support networks can be obtained on subscription from Contact a Family, 209-211 City Road, London, EC1V 1JN. Tel: 020-76088700.

BOOKS FOR ADULTS

● Speechmark Publishing Limited provide practical resources for special needs specialists. Their catalogue contains a range of books, including the *Early Skills* series with titles such as *Early Listening Skills*. Other resources include *ColorCards* – photographic language cards on themes such as 'Daily living'. Speechmark Publishing Limited, Telford Road, Bicester, Oxfordshire OX26 4LQ. Tel: 01869-244644.

● *More Quality Circle Time* by Jenny Mosley (Learning Development Aids). Contains ideas on using circle time in nursery and reception, including puppets, drama and guided imagery. Available from LDA, Duke Street, Wisbech, Cambridgeshire PE13 2AE. Tel: 01945-463441.

● *Behaviour in Pre-school Groups* by Ann Henderson (Pre-school Learning Alliance). Available from PLA, 69 Kings Cross Road, London WC1X 9LL. Tel: 020-78330991.

● *Developing Individual Behaviour Plans in Early Years Settings* by Hannah Mortimer (National Association for Special Educational Needs). Available from NASEN, 4-5 Amber Business Village, Amber Close, Amington, Tamworth, Staffordshire B77 4RP. Tel: 01827-311500.

● *Positive Parenting* by Frank Merrett (Quality for Effective Development). Available from QEd, The Rom Building, Eastern Avenue, Lichfield WS13 6RN. Tel: 01543-416353.

● *Confident Children: Developing Your Child's Self-esteem* by Glen Stenhouse (Oxford University Press)

● *The Music Makers Approach: Inclusive Activities for Young Children with Special*

Educational Needs by Hannah Mortimer (NASEN) (address above).

● *Index for Inclusion: Developing Learning and Participation in Schools* by Booth, Ainscow, Black-Hawkins, Vaughan and Shaw (CSIE). Obtainable from the Centre for Studies on Inclusive Education, Room 2S203, 5 Block, Frenchay Campus, Coldharbour Lane, Bristol BS16 1QU. Tel: 0117-9238450. Step-by-step considerations for a setting looking towards developing inclusion.

● *What Works in Inclusive Education?* by Judy Sebba and Darshan Sachdev (Barnardo's)

BOOKS FOR CHILDREN

● The Magination Press specializes in books which help young children to deal with personal or psychological concerns. Send for a catalogue from The Eurospan Group, 3 Henrietta Street, Covent Garden, London WC2E 8LU. Tel: 020-72400856.

● *Where the Wild Things Are* by Maurice Sendak (Bodley Head). A classic story on the theme of mischief.

● *Since Dad Left* by Caroline Binch (Frances Lincoln). Coping with family separation.

● *The Second Princess* by Hiawyn Oram and Tony Ross (Anderson Press). Sibling rivalry and sharing.

WEBSITES

● The Department for Education and Employment (D*f*EE) (for parent information and for Government circulars and advice including the SEN *Code of Practice*): www.dfee.gov.uk.

● The National Autistic Society: www.oneworld.org/autism_uk/nas

● The Writers' Press, USA, publish a number of books for young children about a range of SEN: www.writerspress.com

● The Mental Health Foundation publish a free information booklet *All about ADHD*: www.mhf.org.uk

EQUIPMENT SUPPLIERS

● LDA (address above) supply the *Circle Time Kit* by Jenny Mosley. It contains puppets, rainstick, magician's cloak and props for making circle time motivating.

● Super Stickers, P.O. Box 55, 4 Balloo Avenue, Bangor, Co. Down BT19 7PJ. Tel: 028-91454344. For reward and motivation.

● Brainwaves, Trewithan Parc, Lostwithiel, Cornwall PL22 0BD. Tel: 01208-873873. Reward sticker albums and so on.

ORGANIZATIONS THAT PROVIDE TRAINING COURSES

● National Children's Bureau, 8 Wakley Street, London EC1V 7QE. Tel: 020-78436000. Many seminars and workshops on children and on SEN.

● Save the Children, 17 Grove Lane, London SE5 8RD. Tel: 020-77035400. Leaflets, books and training on a wide range of issues including SEN.